ARTHUR C. NELSON
and ROBERT E. LANG

The New Politics of Planning

How States and Local Governments Are Coming to Common Ground on Reshaping America's Built Environment

Urban Land Institute

ABOUT THE URBAN LAND INSTITUTE

The mission of the Urban Land Institute is to provide leadership in the responsible use of land and in creating and sustaining thriving communities worldwide. ULI is committed to

• Bringing together leaders from across the fields of real estate and land use policy to exchange best practices and serve community needs;

• Fostering collaboration within and beyond ULI's membership through mentoring, dialogue, and problem solving;

• Exploring issues of urbanization, conservation, regeneration, land use, capital formation, and sustainable development;

• Advancing land use policies and design practices that respect the uniqueness of both built and natural environments;

• Sharing knowledge through education, applied research, publishing, and electronic media; and

• Sustaining a diverse global network of local practice and advisory efforts that address current and future challenges.

Established in 1936, the Institute today has more than 40,000 members worldwide, representing the entire spectrum of the land use and development disciplines. ULI relies heavily on the experience of its members. It is through member involvement and information resources that ULI has been able to set standards of excellence in development practice. The Institute has long been recognized as one of the world's most respected and widely quoted sources of objective information on urban planning, growth, and development.

Richard M. Rosan
President, ULI Worldwide

ULI PROJECT STAFF

Rachelle Levitt
Executive Vice President
Global Information Group

Dean Schwanke
Senior Vice President
Publications and Awards

Nancy H. Stewart
Director, Book Program

James A. Mulligan
Managing Editor

Laura Glassman, Publications
  Professionals LLC
Manuscript Editor

Betsy VanBuskirk
Creative Director

Anne Morgan
Graphic Design

Craig Chapman
Director, Publishing Operations

AUTHORS

Arthur C. Nelson
Presidential Professor and Director of
  Metropolitan Research
University of Utah
Salt Lake City, Utah

Robert E. Lang
Professor and Director
Metropolitan Institute at Virginia Tech
Alexandria, Virginia

Recommended bibliographic listing:
Nelson, Arthur C., and Robert E. Lang. *The New Politics of Planning: How States and Local Governments Are Coming to Common Ground on Reshaping America's Built Environment*. Washington, D.C.: ULI–the Urban Land Institute, 2009.

ULI Order #N33
ISBN 978-0-87420-128-4

©2009 by the Urban Land Institute
1025 Thomas Jefferson Street, N.W.
Suite 500 West
Washington, D.C. 20007-5201

Contents

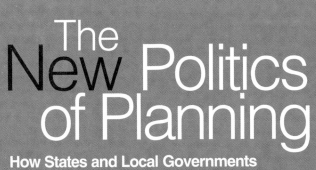

The
New Politics
of Planning

**How States and Local Governments
Are Coming to Common Ground on Reshaping
America's Built Environment**

Introduction

By 2025, the U.S. population will approach 350 million, adding 67 million people since 2000 (U.S. Census Bureau 2005). No quarter century of the nation's history will have seen such population growth. The nation will need 35 million new housing units to accommodate this expansion. Another 17 million homes must be rebuilt, replaced, or substantially renovated, bringing the total number of units constructed to about 52 million, or about 45 percent of the 116 million units that existed in 2000 (Nelson 2006).

During the same period, the United States will also add about 26 million jobs, requiring 15 billion square feet more nonresidential space than the 81 billion existing in 2000. Because nonresidential space is less durable than residential space, another 63 billion square feet of nonresidential space must be replaced, rebuilt, or substantially renovated, bringing the total space constructed to 78 billion square feet—or nearly what existed in 2000 (Nelson 2006).

The bottom line is that the United States will see about $30 trillion in development between 2000 and 2025. Goetz (2007, 20) notes that each state will need to recognize that new development "will help determine the future quality of life of its residents, its economic growth prospects, and its attractiveness to domestic migrants and foreign immigrants."

This report for the Urban Land Institute looks back at efforts during the past generation to manage growth. It also assesses recent trends and offers a read on the future. It begins with a compact history of land use controls in the United States, progresses into the era called the "quiet revolution" in land use control (from the late 1960s into the late 1990s), reviews what some have called the "not-so-quiet revolution" in land use controls that began about the middle 1980s, and moves into what we label the "new dialogue" that has emerged in the early 21st century.[1]

Overarching the eras is an evolving interaction between respect for property rights, on the one hand, and the need to address the externalities of land development, on the other. Property rights are broadly (though rarely completely) understood by most Americans, but the concept of externalities is elusive. A new development that reduces one's property value may be called a "negative" externality, but if it raises one's property value, it would be viewed as a "positive" externality. Local government policy tends to be preoccupied with preventing or mitigating negative externalities, thus the term "externality" itself has come to mean only negative impacts, not positive ones. Over the past generation, tension has existed about how to balance property rights with mitigating externalities. Emerging trends indicate less direct state-level influence in local government planning affairs and some important restrictions, yet also some important new powers. A new dialogue may be attempting to balance competing interests. Before we address features of the new dialogue, a brief review of the history of land use controls in the United States is useful.

A Brief History of Land Use Controls

James C. Nicholas (1999) offers as succinct a review of American land use control history as anyone, and we paraphrase his work extensively. Nicholas observes that from the beginning of statehood, states had the authority to control land use but typically chose to delegate that control to local government. For their part, many local governments chose not to exercise their authority or, if so, in limited respects only. The discerning reader is referred to more detailed historical treatment by John Reps (1966).

In truth, the idea of regulating development through land use controls is a relatively new concept. Nicholas notes, however, that planning in some form has been practiced in the United States since before the country's founding. Philadelphia and Savannah were new towns planned a century before the American Revolution. Land use controls emerged as villages grew into large cities. New York City enacted legislation addressing tenements in 1867. Larger cities followed New York's example by enacting sanitation and building codes for new construction throughout the latter half of the 19th century. New York City adopted the nation's first comprehensive zoning code in 1916, still less than a century ago. It addressed the type, location, and use of buildings that could be constructed within zoning districts. Nicholas observes that:

> Zoning was the beginning of the end for the laissez-faire approach to urban planning. Prior to zoning, community plans simply expressed the desires of the community; however, the individual property owner was free to reject these desires. Community plans would now be expressed in the negative through zoning. (Nicholas 1999, 1)

Controlling land use through zoning was not without controversy. It was, however, a pragmatic solution to the nation's growth. The 1920 census found that for the first time statistically more Americans lived in urban than in rural places. That percentage now exceeds 80 percent—and with the inclusion of the new "micropolitan area" designation, only 7 percent of Americans live in census-defined "non-core-based areas." Nicholas (1999, 1) observes that "[a]s Americans urbanized, they began living closer to one another, following industrial rather than agricultural pursuits. Land and land use concerns naturally turned from a frontier-agricultural setting to an urban-industrial setting."

These developments led the U.S. Supreme Court in the 1920s to issue three decisions important to planning. In 1926, the Court held that the regulation of land use was a constitutionally sanctioned form of the police power.[2] Nevertheless, the

Court found in 1928 that land use regulatory authority was subject to restrictions and limitations.[3] Earlier in the decade, in 1922, the Court held that land use regulation may result in the taking of private property without just compensation.[4]

Against the legal backdrop was the reality that the United States in the early 20th century was becoming an urban nation. Urbanizing local governments struggled with conflicting planning authority, unclear delegations of power from states, and growing federal court interest in land use regulation. This situation led to the Standard State Zoning Enabling Act (SSZEA), crafted by the U.S. Department of Commerce. As a model act, versions of the SSZEA were eventually adopted by all 50 states. Much has changed since the SSZEA was drafted, however.

Although the SSZEA was principally intended to enable regulation of land uses, it had important planning purposes as well. This goal is seen in its mission, which states that municipalities may regulate structures and land "[f]or the purpose of promoting health, safety, morals, or the general welfare of the community," and that

> [s]uch regulations shall be made in accordance with a *comprehensive plan* and designed to lessen congestion in the streets; to secure safety from fire, panic, and other dangers; to promote health and the general welfare; to provide adequate light and air; to prevent the overcrowding of land; to avoid undue concentration of population; *to facilitate the adequate provision of transportation, water, sewerage, schools, parks, and other public requirements.* (Nicholas 1999, 1; emphasis added)

Whether for regulating land uses or planning to meet future needs, however, the one overarching principle of planning and zoning is to prevent "negative externalities." An externality occurs when action on one property affects another. If a park is constructed near homes, residents of the homes may benefit from the open spaces, recreation opportunities, and other forms of "positive" externalities. If the land is developed as a solid waste transfer station, however, negative externalities can occur associated with truck traffic, unsightliness, and unkempt conditions. In both cases, the externalities occur internal to a community.

What if the negative externality is caused by another community, or even another state, outside the reach of the affected one? A classic example would be smoke traveling from one community to another. The problem is that the host community has little incentive to reduce smoke if its economic livelihood depends on the business producing it. The affected community may have no authority to change the host jurisdiction's behavior and thus may need to turn to higher authorities, including even the federal government.

By the 1970s, the SSZEA was seen as mostly incapable of addressing externalities occurring between communities, including states. A "new mood" took hold, as eloquently exposited by William Reilly, the first director of the president's Council on Environmental Quality:

> There is a new mood in America. Increasingly citizens are asking what urban growth will add to the quality of their lives. They are questioning the way relatively unconstrained, piecemeal urbanization is changing their communities and are rebelling against the traditional processes of government and the marketplace which, they believe, have inadequately guided development in the past. They are measuring new development proposals by the extent to which environmental criteria are satisfied—by what new housing and business will generate in terms of additional traffic, pollution of air and water, erosion and scenic disturbance. (William Reilly, as quoted in Nelson and Duncan 1995, 1)

State efforts to manage urban development in light of the new mood were researched and published by Fred Bosselman and David Callies (1971) in a work titled *The Quiet Revolution in Land Use Control.* Included in their review were the Hawaiian Land Use Law, Maine Site Location Law, Massachusetts Wetlands Protection Program, Massachusetts Zoning Appeals Law, New England River Basins Commission, San Francisco Bay Conservation and Development Commission, Twin Cities Metropolitan Council, Vermont Environmental Control Law, and Wisconsin Shoreland Protection Program.

The Council on Environmental Quality commissioned this work to review innovative state land use laws for their application to President Nixon's proposed National Land Use Policy Act of 1971. The bill, which was never adopted, would have had states identify and control development in areas of critical environmental concern, manage developments of regional impact, and ensure that developments of regional benefit would not be unduly restricted by local governments. Some of these innovations were implemented in Florida's Environmental Land and Water Management Act (1972), which required the state to manage development in areas of critical state concern and introduced developments of regional impact into the regulatory landscape of the state. Ultimately, "quiet revolution" was an apt label, given their findings—"quiet" because these innovative laws were passed without much fanfare or coordinated effort by the states, and "revolution" because so many states had embarked on state-level efforts to intervene in local land use planning and decision-making processes to exercise broad state interests that it changed the state/local relationship that had existed since the SSZEA.

The quiet revolution gave way to one that was "not so quiet" (Weitz 1999), involving several states that embarked on ambitious statewide planning and land use regulatory campaigns. Those efforts started in roughly the early 1970s and extended about 20 years into the 1990s. Leading states in this movement included Colorado, Connecticut, Florida, Maine, Oregon, Rhode Island, Vermont, and Washington (Gale 1992). Most state efforts were characterized as having strong state influence in local planning but were accomplished through a state/local partnership in which states established goals and objectives while local governments prepared plans showing how state interests would be achieved (Weitz 1999).

Table 1 summarizes many but not all significant state-level land use acts after the quiet revolution approximately began. Four books provide important insights into the politics of statewide land use planning policies over the past generation, beginning with Frank J. Popper's *The Politics of Land Use Reform* (1981), and followed by John M. Degrove's three books published in successive decades: *Land, Growth and Politics* (1984), *The New Frontier for Land Policy* (DeGrove and Miness 1992), and *Planning Policy and Politics: Smart Growth and the States* (2005).

Many of the efforts pursued in some states have created a backlash. Colorado, Connecticut, and Maine scaled back state-level roles within a few years of legislative adoption. Florida and Oregon have seen important property rights initiatives curtail some elements of planning. At the same time, use of "ballot box planning" has grown, as well as state acts that enable more creative planning and broadening participation in land use planning processes. Although the private sector has always had significant involvement in activities that influence planning, what is emerging is the growing influence of private nonprofit organizations such as land trusts. The United States is now in a new era of planning we call the new dialogue. The reasoning and evidence for this conclusion are now offered.

Table 1. State Land Use Planning Laws

State	Year	Title	Law
Arizona	1998	Growing Smarter Act, transfer development rights act	S. 1238, Ch. 145
	2000	Growing Smarter Plus Act	
Delaware	2001	Comprehensive Plans and Annexation Law	H.B. 255
		Planning Coordination	S.B. 105
		Graduated Impact Fees	H.B. 235
		Reality Transfer Tax for Conservation Trust Fund	H.B. 192
Florida	1972	Environmental Land and Water Management Act	Fla. Stat. 380 et seq.
	1975	Local Government Comprehensive Planning Act	
	1984–85	Omnibus Growth Management Act	
	2003	Pay as You Grow	
	2005	Growth management amendments	
Georgia	1989	Coordinated Planning Legislation	O.C.G.A. 50-8-1 et seq.
	1992	Amendments to Planning Law	
Hawaii	1961	Hawaii Land Use Law	Hawaii Rev. Stats., Ch. 205
	1978	Hawaii State Plan	Act 100
Louisiana	2004	Neighborhood Enhancement Program	H.B. 1720
Maine	1988	Comprehensive Planning and Land Use Regulation Act	30 M.R.S.A. Sec. 4960
Maryland	1992	Economic Growth, Resource Protection, and Planning Act	
	1997	Smart Growth Areas Act	
	2001	GreenPrint Program	H.B. 1379
New Hampshire	2000	Smart Growth Bill	H.B. 1259
New Jersey	1985	State Planning Act	NJSA 52-18A-196 et seq.
	1999	Smart Growth Planning Grants	
	2001	State Development and Redevelopment Plan	
	2005	Smart Growth Tax Credit Act	A.B. 1356
Oregon	1973	Land Conservation and Development Act	S.B. 100, Oregon Stats. 197
Pennsylvania	2000	Growth Area Legislation, transfer development rights	H.B. 14 (Act 67); S.B. 300 (Act 68)
Rhode Island	1988	Comprehensive Planning and Land Use Regulation Act	Rhode Island General Laws, Ch. 45–22
	2000	Referendums on developer rights, open space	
Tennessee	1998	Growth Policy Law	Public Chapter 1101
Vermont	1970	Environmental Control Act	Act 250, 10 Vermont Stats. 151
	1988	Growth Management Act	Act 200, 24 Vermont Stats. 117
	1990	Amendments to Ch. 117	Act 280
Washington	1990	Growth Management Act	Sub. House Bill 2929
	1991	Amendments to 1990 Growth Management Act	H.B. 1025
Wisconsin	1999	Amendments to local planning enabling laws (commonly referred to as the "smart growth law")	Act 9

Source: Adapted from Gray (2007).

Toward a New Dialogue

A new dialogue appears to be evolving on at least six fronts:

■ States are converging on roughly common approaches to addressing similar issues despite appearances to the contrary.

■ Voters are increasingly willing to raise their taxes to pay for smart growth–related commitments ranging from public transit to open-space preservation to affordable housing production—and the incidence of adoption appears to be nonpartisan in support.

■ Perhaps recognizing that public land use decisions based on smart growth principles may reduce property values based on previous public decisions, several states are considering and some have adopted measures to compensate property owners more broadly than may have been the case historically.

■ Private, nonprofit land use actions show promise as a means to dominate patterns of development if sustained over time—thus potentially leaving state and local governments powerless to address some issues.

■ Selected case studies show where states may be converging on common ground in addressing planning issues, albeit through different approaches.

■ Private government has increased explosively in the past three decades, including a rise in homeowners associations (HOAs) and special taxing districts. These are highly localized efforts to address problems that general local government agencies do not or cannot handle because of financial restrictions, enabling restrictions, or both. This trend may be explained in part as an effort to focus management of some government-like functions at the level closest to citizens as consumers of government services. Special districts are increasing in number across the United States (see also Chapin and Thomas 2004). More interesting perhaps is that private governments in the form of HOAs are altering the local regulatory landscape in significant ways and are substituting for local municipal functions such as code enforcement (Lang and LeFurgy 2007). Because private governments derive their rules from common boilerplate language, they are often similar from state to state and are further fueling the convergence of local land use regulation.

The report now examines each of these areas.

A New Convergence

Two broad eras of state convergence exist in planning and environmental policy. The first is the SSZEA—adopted in whole or in substantial part by all states over a period of about 20 years. The second is the National Environmental Policy Act of 1970—versions of which were adopted by about half the states, leading to state-level, project-specific environmental review (through "mini-environmental impact statements") or the broadening of state interests in local environment-related decision making.

The United States may be entering an era of new convergence. We hypothesize that states generally are converging in their overall statewide planning efforts—that is, states that may have lagged in some respects a generation ago have improved their efforts, whereas states that made significant efforts a generation ago have not advanced. The convergence is thus related to some lagging states moving up and advanced states holding steady. We make this claim by establishing a baseline reflecting laws and conditions reported during the period 1983 through 1991 and then comparing it to planning laws in effect into 2005.

The baseline is constructed from state rankings developed by two studies that assessed state-level environmental and planning laws, and by implication laws affecting development roughly a generation ago. The first study, by Christopher Duerksen (1983), evaluated state laws along 23 dimensions, including one that addressed political characteristics (such as Democratic or Republican representation in Congress). States were ranked from most favorable toward environmental protection (Minnesota) to least favorable (Alabama). A decade later, Bob Hall and Mary Lee Kerr (1991) published their "green index" based on 179 indicators of environmental conditions, ranking states from best (California) to worst (Wyoming). For the most part, these studies ranked states comparably (Meyer 1995), as shown in Table 2. We combine the ranks of these studies to create a baseline rank of states' environmental and planning efforts and environmental conditions of a generation ago.

In 2002, the American Planning Association (APA) published its *Growing Smart Legislative Guidebook* (Meck 2002). The APA guidebook included a compendium of state planning legislation focusing on planning rigor (such as whether plans were mandatory and included state-level review) and content (such as mandatory or optional planning elements). We created an index and ranked the states based on overall planning commitment (Table 3).

Table 4 compares the change in state rankings between the baseline and current conditions. The one thing that is striking is that several states at the bottom of the baseline rankings did more to advance planning through state policy between the baseline period and this decade. For example, whereas Mississippi ranked last in the baseline ranking for the period 1983 to 1991, by 2002 it ranked 25th in planning effort—a shift of 25 places. Idaho had the largest shift—from 43rd to eighth, a change of 35 places—followed by Nevada, which moved up 33 places from 45th to 12th. Utah shifted from 38th to ninth, or 29 places, and Georgia climbed 25 places, from 28th to third. Other notable advances were recorded by Arizona and West Virginia, which shifted 18 places, with Louisiana shifting 17 places, Kentucky 16, and Arkansas shifting 15.

Planning laws and environmental laws do not necessarily converge, however. For this reason, we combine the baseline ranks with the APA-derived ranks (unweighted) to generate a composite rank that includes both elements, shown in Table 4. This table shows some of the "usual suspects" at the top of the combined rankings, such as Oregon, Florida, and California, which take the top three spots. Some other states emerge among the new leaders, however, such as Arizona, Georgia, Kentucky, Montana, Utah, and Wisconsin.

Several caveats are in order. First, the baseline and APA-derived rankings compare many different things: combining them is interesting, but the results should not be given undue importance. Second, the figures are not weighted to refine the influence of one factor over another; all factors are given equal weight. Third, just because laws and policies are on the books does not mean outcomes are tied to them. Georgia, for example, is tied for third with Oregon in the Nelson-Lang ranking because of the content of its state planning laws, yet its environmental and other quality-of-life outcomes lag far behind those of the Pacific Northwest state (see Nelson 2000).

Also note that the convergence is not widespread. Several states have not converged as rapidly as others, such as Alabama, North Dakota, Texas, and Wyoming. Nonetheless, we surmise from this exercise that lower-ranked states have been comparatively more active than higher-ranked ones in advancing planning and environmental laws; the convergence in this respect is mostly movement of lower-ranked states toward the mean. Another kind of convergence—dealing with property rights and overall state-level rigor in overseeing local planning—is reviewed in a later section.

Table 2. Baseline Rank by State of Environmental and Planning Laws and Environmental Conditions, 1983–1991

State	Duerksen Index Rank, 1983	Green Index Rank, 1991	Combined Rank Score	Composite Rank
Alabama	50	46	96	49
Alaska	34	45	79	41
Arizona	33	32	65	34
Arkansas	27	48	75	37
California	2	1	3	1
Colorado	28	30	58	31
Connecticut	15	5	20	8
Delaware	22	29	51	27
Florida	18	7	25	11
Georgia	30	24	54	28
Hawaii	13	25	38	17
Idaho	47	34	81	43
Illinois	24	15	39	19
Indiana	12	27	39	18
Iowa	22	12	34	16
Kansas	34	31	65	33
Kentucky	13	36	49	26
Louisiana	44	47	91	48
Maine	15	14	29	13
Maryland	8	13	21	9
Massachusetts	4	4	8	3
Michigan	19	11	30	14
Minne sota	1	8	9	4
Mississippi	48	49	97	50
Missouri	49	28	77	39
Montana	8	33	41	23

State	Duerksen Index Rank, 1983	Green Index Rank, 1991	Combined Rank Score	Composite Rank
Nebraska	40	23	63	32
Nevada	40	43	83	45
New Hampshire	6	18	24	10
New Jersey	3	3	6	2
New Mexico	46	39	85	47
New York	8	9	17	7
North Carolina	30	10	40	21
North Dakota	40	40	80	42
Ohio	19	22	41	22
Oklahoma	45	37	82	44
Oregon	5	6	11	6
Pennsylvania	24	21	45	25
Rhode Island	28	17	45	24
South Carolina	30	26	56	29
South Dakota	19	38	57	30
Tennessee	34	41	75	35
Texas	40	35	75	36
Utah	34	42	76	38
Vermont	15	19	34	15
Virginia	24	16	40	20
Washington	7	20	27	12
West Virginia	34	44	78	40
Wisconsin	8	2	10	5
Wyoming	34	50	84	46

Sources: Duerksen Index Rank based on Duerksen (1983); Green Index Rank based on Hall and Kerr (1991).
Rankings are not based on weighted factors.

Table 3. Ranking of States by Planning Rigor and Content, 2002

State	Plan Mandated	State Land Use Policy Basis	Strength of State Role	Internal Consistency Required	Structure Score	Total Elements	Total Score	Nelson-Lang Rank
Alabama	1		1		2	4	6	41
Alaska	3		2		5	4	9	31
Arizona	1		1		2	12	14	16
Arkansas	2	1	2		5	6	11	22
California	3		2	1	6	9	15	12
Colorado	1		1		2	4	6	41
Connecticut	1		2		3	12	15	12
Delaware	3	1	3	1	8	11	19	5
Florida	3	1	3	1	8	15	23	1
Georgia	3	1	3	1	8	12	20	3
Hawaii	3	1	3		7	5	12	20
Idaho	3		2		5	12	17	8
Illinois	2		1		3	5	8	36
Indiana	1		1		2	7	9	31
Iowa	2		1		3	7	10	25
Kansas	2		1		3	6	9	31
Kentucky	3		2	1	6	10	16	10
Louisiana	1		1		2	7	9	31
Maine	1	1	3	1	6	10	16	10
Maryland	1	1	3	1	6	7	13	18
Massachusetts	3		2	1	6	8	14	16
Michigan	1		1		2	6	8	36
Minnesota	1		2		3	7	10	25
Mississippi	1		2		3	7	10	25
Missouri	1		1		2	4	6	41
Montana	1		1		2	9	11	22
Nebraska	3		2		5	3	8	36
Nevada	3		2		5	10	15	12
New Hampshire	1	1	3		5	7	12	20
New Jersey	2		2		4	9	13	18
New Mexico	1		1		2	3	5	47
New York	2		2		4	11	15	12

State	Plan Mandated	State Land Use Policy Basis	Strength of State Role	Internal Consistency Required	Structure Score	Total Elements	Total Score	Nelson-Lang Rank
North Carolina	2		1		3	0	3	49
North Dakota	2		1		3	5	8	36
Ohio	1		1		2	4	6	41
Oklahoma	1		1		2	4	6	41
Oregon	3	1	3	1	8	12	20	3
Pennsylvania	1		2		3	7	10	25
Rhode Island	3	1	3	1	8	10	18	6
South Carolina	1		2		3	7	10	25
South Dakota	3		2		5	4	9	31
Tennessee	1		1		2	5	7	40
Texas	2		1		3	1	4	49
Utah	2		2		4	13	17	9
Vermont	1	1	3		5	13	18	7
Virginia	1		1		2	8	10	25
Washington	3	1	3	1	8	14	22	2
West Virginia	1		2		3	8	11	22
Wisconsin	1		1		2	4	6	41
Wyoming	1		1		2	3	5	47

Source: Adapted by the authors from Meck (2002).

Note: Column definitions (for details on APA's approach, see the two-volume publication):

Plan Mandated—From Meck (2002) table 7.5: 3 = mandated plan; 2 = mandated plan if jurisdiction meets certain conditions (such as having a planning commission, being a certain size or growth rate, or other factors); 1 = optional, that is, plan simply being enabled.

State Land Use Policy Basis—From Meck (2002) table 7.5: where 1 = yes; blank = no.

Strength of State Role—From Meck (2002) table 7.5: 3 = strong (such as state review and approval of plans before being eligible for certain state programs); 2 = significant (such as state review and approval in an advisory capacity or limited if any loss of eligibility for certain state programs); 1 = weak (no state review).

Internal Consistency Required—From Meck (2002) table 7.5: 1 = yes; blank = no.

Structure Score—Unweighted sum of the preceding columns.

Total Elements—The number of elements mandated, mandated if conditions are met, or optional through enablement regardless of the rigor needed to address the element. (There are 20 standard elements considered: land use, growth limits, housing, economic development, agriculture/forest/open-space land preservation, critical and sensitive areas, natural hazards, redevelopment, recreation, energy, air quality, transportation, community facilities, human services, community design, historic preservation, implementation, policy, visioning or public participation, and local coordination.)

Total Score—Sum of structure score and total elements.

Nelson-Lang Rank—Rank of state by total score with 1 being the highest and 49 (because of ties) being lowest.

Table 4. Change between Baseline and Current Rankings, and Overall Combined Ranks

State	Baseline Rank	Nelson-Lang Rank	Difference (Baseline Minus Nelson-Lang)	Change in Rank Order	Baseline Plus Nelson-Lang Rank	Overall Combined Rank
Alaska	41	31	10	13	72	39
Arizona	34	16	18	7	50	25
Arkansas	37	22	15	12	59	32
California	1	12	–11	40	13	3
Colorado	31	41	–10	38	72	39
Connecticut	8	12	–4	31	20	7
Delaware	27	5	22	6	32	16
Florida	11	1	10	13	12	2
Georgia	28	3	25	4	31	15
Hawaii	17	20	–3	30	37	18
Idaho	43	8	35	1	51	28
Illinois	19	36	–17	45	55	30
Indiana	18	31	–13	41	49	24
Iowa	16	25	–9	36	41	19
Kansas	33	31	2	23	64	36
Kentucky	26	10	16	11	36	17
Louisiana	48	31	17	10	79	44
Maine	13	10	3	20	23	10
Maryland	9	18	–9	36	27	11
Massachusetts	3	16	–13	41	19	5
Michigan	14	36	–22	48	50	25
Minnesota	4	25	–21	47	29	12
Mississippi	50	25	25	4	75	31
Missouri	39	41	–2	29	80	45
Montana	23	22	1	24	45	20

State	Baseline Rank	Nelson-Lang Rank	Difference (Baseline Minus Nelson-Lang)	Change in Rank Order	Baseline Plus Nelson-Lang Rank	Overall Combined Rank
Nebraska	32	36	−4	31	68	37
Nevada	45	12	33	2	57	31
New Hampshire	10	20	−10	38	30	13
New Jersey	2	18	−16	44	20	7
New Mexico	47	47	0	25	94	50
New York	7	12	−5	33	19	5
North Carolina	21	49	−28	49	70	38
North Dakota	42	36	6	18	78	43
Ohio	22	41	−19	46	63	35
Oklahoma	44	41	3	20	85	45
Oregon	6	3	3	20	9	1
Pennsylvania	25	25	0	25	50	25
Rhode Island	24	6	18	7	30	13
South Carolina	29	25	4	19	54	29
South Dakota	30	31	−1	27	61	33
Tennessee	35	40	−5	33	75	41
Texas	36	49	−13	41	85	45
Utah	38	9	29	3	47	23
Vermont	15	7	8	16	22	9
Virginia	20	25	−5	33	45	20
Washington	12	2	10	13	14	4
West Virginia	40	22	18	7	62	34
Wisconsin	5	41	−36	50	46	22
Wyoming	46	47	−1	27	93	49

Source: Compiled from Tables 2 and 3 by the authors.

Voter Willingness to Raise Taxes

The progression in state land use planning has been accompanied by the increasing willingness of voters to raise taxes for a variety of transit, open-space, and related smart growth initiatives. Table 5 illustrates this trend from 1994 to 2006. New spending obligations adopted through the ballot box span the range from preservation of open space to construction of light-rail transit. Although some are statewide in scope, most are regional, such as for light rail, or local, such as for open-space acquisition.

Clearly, voters favor various smart growth initiatives, passing more than three-quarters of them from 1994 to 2006, generating more than $110 billion in revenues in 2007 dollars. More than 80 percent of the tax increases were imposed on real property, with much of the rest involving increased sales taxes. The rate of adoption is high, probably because interest-group polling and focus-group analysis both indicate the general level of support for ballot measures and often ignore the nuances of ballot measure language. The choice of financing scheme is usually limited by state statutes and constitutions to just the property tax or sometimes the sales tax.

Worth noting are the new light-rail projects that have passed in what once appeared to be the most transit-averse states, such as those in the Mountain West. Rail projects are now funded, operating, or under construction in Arizona, Colorado, and Utah. In fact, the Denver region is building the largest light-rail system in the United States, while Salt Lake City is significantly expanding its transit and adding commuter-rail lines at the same time. For their book *Boomburbs: The Rise of America's Accidental Cities*, Lang and LeFurgy (2007) interviewed planners, developers, and elected officials in all three states and found a remarkable degree of bipartisan support not only for rail, but also for the denser transit-oriented development that accompanies it. For example, Daybreak, a new urbanist development designed by Peter Calthorpe for a subsidiary of Kennecott Utah Copper in the Salt Lake Valley, agreed to add 6,000 new condominium and apartment units within a quarter mile of light-rail stations planned to serve the development, thereby increasing Daybreak's overall inventory of residential units from 14,000 to 20,000.

Year	Measures	Passed	Percentage Passed	Funds Approved (billions of 2007 dollars)
1994	50	33	66	$1.45
1995	42	34	81	$1.67
1996	96	68	71	$6.88
1997	80	67	84	$3.32
1998	175	143	82	$9.10
1999	107	95	89	$3.05
2000	209	171	82	$13.60
2001	197	137	70	$2.19
2002	192	143	74	$9.84
2003	133	99	74	$1.92
2004	219	164	75	$28.58
2005	140	111	79	$2.84
2006	180	134	74	$29.68
Total	**1,820**	**1,399**	**77**	**$114.10**
Average	140	108	77	$16.30

Source: Calculated by the authors from the Trust for Public Land, Conservation Finance Program Land Vote Database, 1994–2006.

Increasing Protections for Private Property Rights

The discussion has another side. Voters and legislatures seem increasingly willing to elevate certain private property rights to a higher level than may have been the case in the past. Emblematic of this new attitude is Oregon's Ballot Measure 37 and the U.S. Supreme Court case *Kelo v. City of New London.*[5]

Efforts to restrict local government authority over land use decisions regarding private property are not new (see Jacobs 2003, 2005), but they have taken a different tack in the very recent past. The leading example is Oregon's Ballot Measure 37, adopted by voters in 2004. Measure 37 allows people whose land would have been eligible for development before land use restrictions were imposed to be compensated for the alleged lost value of the land or to have current regulations waived in favor of prior regulations. Several states have considered similar ballot measures since then; about half have been approved. (More discussion of Measure 37 is provided in the later section on Oregon.)

Kelo was a 2005 U.S. Supreme Court case decided by a 5–4 margin, upholding as constitutional the use of eminent domain to transfer land from one private owner to another to further economic development. Since that decision, several states, through either legislative action or the ballot box, have restricted such private-to-private condemnations. Some have gone further in restricting the ability of local governments to engage in urban renewal, redevelopment, or even acquisition of private land for such public purposes as roads, schools, and parks.

Generally, ballot measures patterned after Oregon's Ballot Measure 37 or attempting to restrict eminent domain in ways the *Kelo* Court found otherwise constitutional fall into five broad categories:

■ Requiring compensation for reduction in property values associated with prior changes in local land use regulations or waiving the applicable regulations;

■ Requiring compensation when local land use regulations reduce property values below a certain threshold;

■ Prohibiting use of eminent domain for selected economic development purposes, to generate tax revenue, or to transfer private property to another private use;

■ Restricting use of eminent domain to blighted properties or to areas where most properties are blighted and other properties are necessary to complete a redevelopment plan; and

■ Increasing the amount of compensation for condemned property that is a person's principal residence over what may have been awarded under previous laws.

The following list summarizes the state-level ballot measures approved or rejected in 2006 alone—after Oregon's Ballot Measure 37 and the *Kelo* decision—that regulate land use or restrict eminent domain. It also includes more general efforts to restrict local government efforts to make land use decisions unless they are accompanied by compensation. Some ballot measures combine *Kelo*-related condemnation restrictions with Ballot Measure 37–style compensation or waiver of enforcement for regulatory barriers adopted in the past that allegedly reduce property values in the present.

■ Arizona: *Passed* citizen initiative prohibiting exercise of eminent domain for private economic development. Also requires compensation to owners when new land use laws decrease their property values.

■ California: *Rejected* citizen initiative that would have restricted eminent domain and amended the state constitution to require compensation for regulatory takings.

■ Florida: *Passed* constitutional amendment approved by legislature banning the use of eminent domain to take private property for private development unless an exemption is approved by three-fifths of both houses of the state legislature.

■ Georgia: *Passed* constitutional amendment approved by legislature prohibiting use of eminent domain for redevelopment except for public use and requiring the approval of the elected city or county governing authority for eminent domain takings.

■ Idaho: *Rejected* citizen initiative that would have prohibited use of eminent domain for private economic development and required local governments to compensate property owners for regulatory takings.

■ Louisiana: *Passed* constitutional amendment prohibiting use of eminent domain for economic development.

■ Michigan: *Passed* constitutional amendment approved by legislature that makes some takings of private property unconstitutional and would require governments to pay property owners more than fair market value.

■ Nevada: *Passed* constitutional amendment initiated by citizens that would prohibit use of eminent domain for economic development and increase compensation for takings. (This measure must be approved again on ballot in 2008 to change the state constitution.)

■ New Hampshire: *Passed* constitutional amendment approved by legislature to ban eminent domain taking of private property for purpose of private development or private use.

■ North Dakota: *Passed* citizen-initiated constitutional amendment prohibiting use of eminent domain for economic development.

■ Oregon: *Passed* citizen initiative banning state and local governments from taking private property for economic development.

■ South Carolina: *Passed* constitutional amendment to prohibit eminent domain takings by state for economic development.

■ Washington: *Rejected* initiative that would have required compensation to property owners for regulations that decrease property values.

The accompanying tables evaluate the political nature of Oregon Ballot Measure 37–style ballot measures addressing land use regulations or restrictions on use of eminent domain.[6] Table 6 summarizes ballot measure votes in 2006 by state and whether land use regulation/eminent domain restriction ballot measures passed or failed. Table 7 reviews the central legislative theme considered in the ballot measures. Table 8 summarizes voting patterns by state and metropolitan area.

Table 6. Summary of Land Use Regulation/Eminent Domain Restriction Votes by State, 2006

State	Ballot/Question/ Initiative Number	Percentage Yes	Percentage No	Passed
Arizona	Proposition 207	65.2	34.8	Yes
California	Proposition 90	47.5	52.5	No
Florida	Constitutional Amendment 8	69.1	30.9	Yes
Georgia	Constitutional Amendment 1	82.6	17.4	Yes
Idaho	Proposition 2	23.9	76.1	No
Louisiana	Constitutional Amendment 4	60.8	39.2	Yes
Michigan	Constitutional Amendment 4	80.1	19.9	Yes
North Dakota	Constitutional Amendment 2	67.6	32.4	Yes
New Hampshire	Constitutional Amendment 1	85.5	14.5	Yes
Nevada	Constitutional Amendment 2	63.1	36.9	Yes
Oregon	Ballot Measure 39	67.0	33.0	Yes
South Carolina	Constitutional Amendment 5	86.0	14.0	Yes
Washington	Initiative Measure 933	41.7	58.3	Yes

Source: Compilation of state election data by Karen Danielsen for the Metropolitan Institute at Virginia Tech, Alexandria.

Table 9 evaluates the distribution of votes for and against the measures based on an urban geography typology developed by the Metropolitan Institute at Virginia Tech (Lang and Sanchez 2007). This table indicates that, generally, support is broad across geographic areas for Oregon Ballot Measure 37–style land use regulation/eminent domain restriction ballot measures, but that such measures tend to have less support in inner suburbs. Perhaps inner suburbs are where local governments face the prospect of needing to redevelop or raise taxes to finance services with an ever-declining value of property.

Table 7. Content of Land Use Regulation/Eminent Domain Restriction Ballot Measures, 2006

State	Eminent Domain	Regulatory Takings	Compensation	Waiver	No Economic Development	Extra Vote
Arizona	X	X	X	X[a]	X	
California	X	X	X		X	
Florida					X	X
Georgia	X[b]				X	X
Idaho	X	X	X		X	
Louisiana	X				X	
Michigan			X[c]			
North Dakota	X				X	
New Hampshire	X				X	
Nevada	X	X	X		X	
Oregon	X				X	
South Carolina	X				X	
Washington		X				

Source: Compilation of state election data by Karen Danielsen, Metropolitan Institute at Virginia Tech, Alexandria.

Notes:

Extra Vote = Vote by state or local legislature needed to allow takings.
No Economic Development = No use of eminent domain for economic development.
a. Waiver is a deed restriction that runs with the land.
b. Use of eminent domain allowed only for public use.
c. Compensation only if taking exceeds fair market value.

Table 8. Land Use Regulation/Eminent Domain Restriction Vote Percentages by State and Metropolitan Area, 2006

State	Metropolitan Area	Percentage Yes	Percentage No
Arizona	Phoenix-Mesa-Scottsdale	66.6	33.4
California	Los Angeles–Long Beach–Santa Ana	47.4	52.6
	Riverside–San Bernardino–Ontario	51.8	48.2
	Sacramento–Arden-Arcade–Roseville	50.1	49.9
	San Diego–Carlsbad–San Marcos	53.8	46.2
	San Francisco–Oakland–Fremont	39.1	60.9
	San Jose–Sunnyvale–Santa Clara	41.7	58.3
Florida	Jacksonville	76.4	23.6
	Miami–Fort Lauderdale–Miami Beach	66.6	33.4
	Orlando	72.5	27.5
	Tampa–St. Petersburg–Clearwater	61.9	38.1
Georgia	Atlanta–Sandy Springs–Marietta	84.3	15.7
Louisiana	New Orleans–Metairie–Kenner	74.8	25.2
Massachusetts	Boston-Cambridge-Quincy, MA-NH	87.5	12.5
Michigan	Detroit-Warren-Livonia	76.5	23.5
Nevada	Las Vegas–Paradise	65.7	34.3
Oregon	Portland-Vancouver-Beaverton, OR-WA	62.3	37.7
South Carolina	Charlotte-Gastonia-Concord, NC-SC	89.7	10.3
Washington	Portland-Vancouver-Beaverton, OR-WA (Vancouver, Washington, voting share)	50.2	49.8
	Seattle-Tacoma-Bellevue	37.1	62.9

Source: Compilation of state election data by the Metropolitan Institute at Virginia Tech, Alexandria.

Table 9. Land Use Regulation/Eminent Domain Restriction Ballot Measure Support by Type, 2006

County Type	Percentage Yes	Percentage No
Core	60.8	39.2
Inner suburbs	50.8	49.2
Mature suburbs	61.0	39.0
Emerging suburbs	65.5	34.5
Exurbs	72.4	27.6

Source: Compilation of state election data by the Metropolitan Institute at Virginia Tech, Alexandria.

The Rise of Private Nonprofit Land Trusts and Public Land Acquisition Programs That Restrict Land Development

Another kind of revolution is occurring in land use management: the rise of private, nonprofit, and selected public measures that effectively take land out of the development supply through acquisition of land or its development rights. Although the 48 contiguous states have about 1.8 billion acres of land, 400 million acres, or about 20 percent, are federally owned. In the West, more than half the total land area is federally owned, and in many of those states, the state itself owns up to half the remaining land, as is the case in Arizona and Oregon. Still, easily more than 1.2 billion acres of land could be available for development. In all, perhaps about 100 million acres of land are actually developed, leaving a supply well in excess of 1 billion acres.[7]

The trouble is that the vast majority of land in private ownership is simply not where urban development occurs. Moreover, much of the land in and near the path of urban development may be removed from the supply of land that may otherwise be developed through a process Mason (2007) calls the "quieter revolution." This withdrawal of land from potential private development occurs when state and local agencies acquire land for a variety of nonurban purposes—such as for watersheds and regional parks, private nonprofit land trusts, federal programs that leverage the purchase of land for conservation and recreation, public acquisition of development rights, dedication of land for nondevelopment uses such as through the land use decision-making process, legal settlements, and numerous other actions. Virtually no accounting exists of the magnitude of land that may be in or near the path of urban development that has been removed from the supply of developable land. We consider three broad efforts.

Interestingly, despite the absence of a coherent federal land use planning scheme, federal land use programs play a much larger role in shaping land use patterns than may be appreciated. One particular initiative is worthy of note: the Land and Water Conservation Fund (LWCF) program.

The LWCF program provides matching grants to states and local governments for the acquisition and development of public outdoor recreation areas and facilities. It is intended to create and maintain a nationwide legacy of high-quality recreation areas and facilities and to stimulate nonfederal investments in the protection and maintenance of recreation resources across the United States. Since 1965, about 40,000 projects have been funded at sites located in nearly all of the nation's 3,141 counties.[8] Over the years, states and local governments have equally matched more than $3.6 billion in federal funds, resulting in the preservation of more than 2.6 million acres of land, averaging about 65,000 acres annually.[9]

Acquisition of development rights—especially rights on agricultural land—is another facet of the quieter revolution. Some states and many local governments throughout the nation purchase development rights to land or allow the "transfer" of development from "sending" to "receiving" areas subject to an overall plan. No complete national inventory exists of the number of acres of land preserved and thus removed from the supply of developable land through these methods. The American Farmland Trust (AFT) published a survey in 2006, estimating that among the "major" government programs more than 1 million acres of development rights had been acquired by local government since 1974 (Sokolow 2006), averaging 30,000 acres annually. Figure 1 shows the jurisdictions in the AFT survey; note that for the most part they are in or near major metropolitan areas.

Private nonprofit land trusts are growing steadily, and with them the amount of land protected from development.[10] Land trusts acquire land or easements on land through purchase, gift, or other means and manage them pursuant to covenants restricting use. These trusts range in landholdings from very large, such as the Trust for Public Land, to the smallest, which preserve perhaps an acre or less of land. They are growing steadily in number and in land controlled, as shown in Figures 2 and 3. Table 10 suggests that the amount of land controlled by trusts has been increasing at a rate of nearly 1.2 million acres annually since 2000.

Table 10. Total Acres Conserved by Local and State Land Trusts, 2000 and 2005

Period	Acres Owned by Land Trusts	Acres under Easement by Land Trusts	Acres Protected by Other Means	Total Acres Conserved
2000	1,219,632	**2,514,545**	2,322,447	6,056,624
2005	1,703,212	**6,245,969**	3,940,928	11,890,109
Increase (acres)	483,580	**3,731,424**	1,618,481	5,833,485
Increase (percent)	40	**148**	70	96

Source: Land Trust Alliance, www.lta.org/census/census_tables.htm (accessed May 30, 2007).

Note: Acres Protected by Other Means includes land protected directly because of activities of the land trust, such as negotiating and preparing for acquisition by other organizations or agencies.

Figure 1. National Assessment of Agricultural Easement Programs

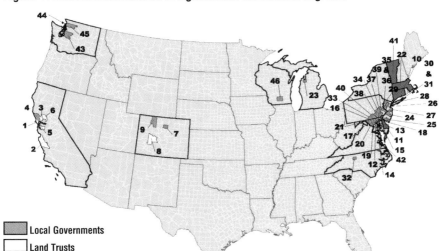

- Local Governments
- Land Trusts
- State Governments

Source: Alvin D. Sokolow, *A National View of Agricultural Easement Programs: Measuring Success in Protecting Farmland–Report 4*, American Farmland Trust and the Agricultural Issues Center of the University of California (Berkeley), December 2006, p.10. http://www.aftresearch.org/research/publications/detail.php?id=b939970b7b60e9da138bcc9164f6ca41z (accessed August 13, 2008).

Figure 2. Growth of Land Trusts, 1950–2005

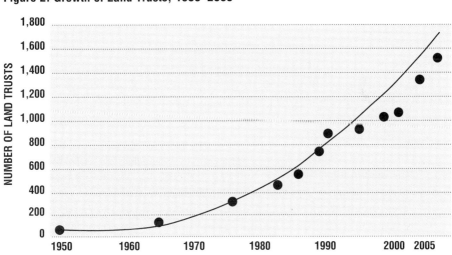

Source: Land Trust Alliance, 2005 National Land Trust Census Tables, www.lta.org/census/census_charts_graphs.htm (accessed June 2, 2007).

Figure 3. Growth in Land Protected from Development, 1985–2005

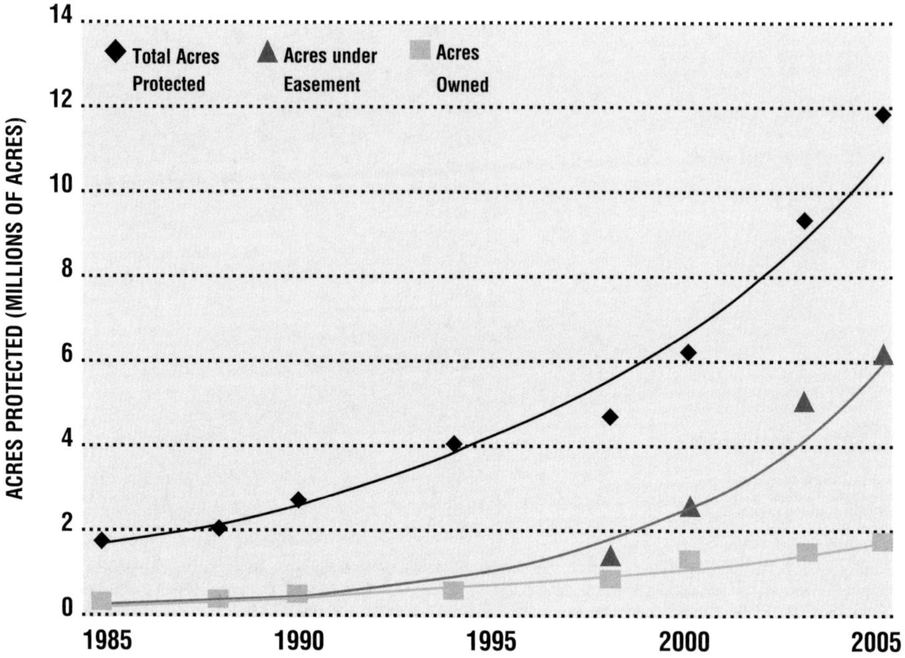

Source: Land Trust Alliance, 2005 National Land Trust Census Tables, www.lta.org/census/census_charts_
graphs.htm (accessed June 2, 2007).

In the range of 1.5 million to 2.0 million, and perhaps more, acres of land—largely in or within commuting distance of metropolitan areas—are being preserved annually. By 2030, the existing base of land protected from development through only the programs and initiatives reviewed above may grow from 10 million acres to perhaps 50 million acres or more, assuming a constant annual rate of protection.

In addition, several states have aggressive land acquisition efforts. Perhaps the leading state initiative is Florida's Preservation 2000/Florida Forever program (Higgins and Paradise 2007). Since 1990, the Florida legislature has spent almost $5 billion on the outright purchase of hundreds of thousands of acres of coastal areas, wetlands, groundwater recharge basins, habitat corridors, and other environmentally sensitive lands. Over decades, the state has acquired more than 6 million acres of conservation lands, spread throughout the state. When combined with federal lands (including military bases) and local governments, Florida has almost 10 million acres managed for a variety of resource protection and resource-based recreation purposes—roughly 30 percent of its total land area. Since 1990, annual land acquisition appropriations have averaged $300 million, and the program was reauthorized in 1999 with broad, bipartisan support (Farr and Brock 2006).

Georgia has a more modest "greenspace" preservation program that started in the early 2000s, but its goal is to preserve at least 20 percent of the state in ecologically viable open spaces (such as habitats linked to each other)—in addition to existing and growing open-space acquisition efforts, such as those for parks and recreation. Maryland has several successful efforts to save open-space land, including the Maryland Agricultural Land Preservation Foundation, which has purchased easements on more than 228,000 acres of land; the Maryland Environmental Trust, which has protected more than 100,000 acres of land; and the Rural Legacy Program, which has purchased over 40,000 acres of rural lands that were under intense development pressure. Mason (2007) notes many other states with similarly aggressive land acquisition programs, focusing mostly in the Northeast.

The Rise of Special Districts and Private Governance

Finally, local government itself appears on the brink of being remade, in part through increasing reliance on special districts and devolution of many local government management responsibilities to homeowners associations—often as a condition of development approval.

Since the Reagan presidency of the 1980s, the federal government has reduced its financial commitment to many state and local governments, notably infrastructure financing, but has not decreased the mandates, such as those relating to water, wastewater, and stormwater treatment quality. Unable to make up for the lost federal funds, states have "passed the buck" to local governments—often increasing their own standards as well. Local governments become trapped with standards to meet but with fewer financial resources. In addition, every state has imposed constraints on state and local taxes over the past generation, thereby reducing local governments' ability to pay for unfunded mandates. To their credit, states have expanded the power of local governments to raise some revenues, such as through impact fees (Newport Partners LLC and Nelson 2007). But one could say that the real "fix" for addressing local infrastructure financing needs is the rise of special districts. In Florida alone, special districts generate well over a billion dollars a year that go toward infrastructure in support of that state's 300,000 net new residents per year (Chapin and Thomas 2007).

As a consequence, local government is a "growth" industry. There is only one federal government, and there has been virtually no change in the number of states (or territories that have since become states) in more than a century. The number of counties has stayed about the same: more than 99 percent of the counties existing in 2002 existed in 1952. The number of cities has risen but only by about 15 percent. Although the number of school districts has fallen to one-fifth the number seen in 1952, the reasons are related to consolidation and efficiency measures discussed later. Special districts, however, have nearly tripled in number, from about 12,000 to 35,000 (Table 11).

Table 11. Governmental Units in the United States, 1952–2002

Type of Government	1952	1962	1972	1982	1992	2002	Total Change 1952–2002
Total Units	116,807	91,237	78,269	81,831	85,006	87,504	–29,303
U.S. Government	1	1	1	1	1	1	0
State Governments	50	50	50	50	50	50	0
Local Governments	116,756	91,186	78,218	81,780	84,955	87,525	–29,231
Counties	3,052	3,043	3,044	3,041	3,043	3,034	–18
Municipalities	16,807	18,000	18,517	19,076	19,279	19,429	2,622
Townships and Towns	17,202	17,142	16,991	16,734	16,656	16,504	–698
School Districts	67,355	34,678	15,781	14,851	14,422	13,506	–53,849
Special Districts	12,340	18,323	23,885	28,078	31,555	35,052	22,712
Local Governments Excluding School Districts	49,401	56,508	62,437	66,929	70,533	74,019	24,618

Source: U.S. Census Bureau, *2002 Census of Governments, Preliminary Report No. 1*, Series GC02-1(P), issued July 2002.
Note: In 1952, Alaska and Hawaii were still territories. They became states in 1959.

Total government employment has been growing at a pace faster than the nation's population. Between 1950 and 2000, the nation's population did not quite double, growing from 150 million to 281 million. Yet total government employment nearly tripled—but not because of federal government growth, which in 2002 was barely more than it was in 1952 (Table 12). State government employment rose fivefold, from about 1.1 million to about 5.1 million. Local government, however, accounted for about half the total change in government employment nationally, growing from 3.5 million to 13.3 million. Local government accounted for a little less than half (48.7 percent) of all employment in 1952, but by 2002, its share had grown to 63.1 percent.

Table 12. Public Employment by Level of Government, 1952–2002

Year	All	Federal	State	Local	Local Government Share (Percent)
1952	7,105,000	2,583,000	1,060,000	3,461,000	48.7
1962	9,388,000	2,539,000	1,680,000	5,169,000	55.1
1972	13,759,000	2,795,000	2,957,000	8,007,000	58.2
1982	15,841,000	2,848,000	3,744,000	9,249,000	58.4
1992	18,164,000	3,047,000	4,587,000	10,531,000	58.0
2002	21,039,000	2,690,000	5,072,000	13,277,000	63.1

Source: U.S. Census Bureau, *2002 Census of Governments, Compendium of Public Employment: 2002*, GC02(3)-2, issued September 2004.

Note: Total for "All" may not match subtotals due to rounding. Figures for all years except 2002 based on October; figures for 2002 based on March.

Why the rapid growth in local governments, especially special districts? There are two main answers. First, people want more things from government than ever before. Second, state and federal governments often find it is in the broad public interest for government to address certain issues—such as water quality, education, and health care—but programs require implementation by local governments. Consider the expansion of special service districts by function over the ten-year period 1992 to 2002 (Table 13). Total special districts increased by 11 percent, or just about the decadal growth rate of 13 percent during the 1990s. An important aspect of this trend is the growing number of highway-toll special districts, which are growing in use in the Southeast (especially Florida, Georgia, and soon Virginia), parts of the West (such as California, Colorado, and soon Arizona), and the Midwest (such as Illinois and Indiana). Another trend is in the growth of multifunction districts, which increased by more than half. For the most part, more special-purpose districts were serving each function in 2002 than in 1992. In contrast, the number of municipalities and counties remained essentially unchanged.

Table 13. Special Service Districts by Function, 1992–2002

Function	1992	2002	Change	Percentage Change
SINGLE-FUNCTION DISTRICTS				
Education	757	518	–239	–31.6
Libraries	1,043	1,580	537	51.5
Hospitals	737	711	–26	–3.5
Health	584	753	169	28.9
Highways	636	743	107	16.8
Airports	435	510	75	17.2
Other Transportation	235	205	–30	–12.8
Fire Protection	5,260	5,725	465	8.8
Drainage and Flood Control	2,709	3,247	538	19.9
Soil and Water Conservation	2,428	2,506	78	3.2
Other Natural Resources	1,091	1,226	135	12.4
Parks and Recreation	1,156	1,287	131	11.3
Housing and Community Development	3,470	3,399	–71	–2.0
Sewerage	1,710	2,004	294	17.2
Solid Waste Management	395	455	60	15.2
Water Supply	3,302	3,406	104	3.1
Other Utilities	461	485	24	5.2
Cemeteries	1,628	1,666	38	2.3
Industrial Development and Mortgage Credit	155	234	79	51.0
Other Single-Function Districts	844	1,161	317	37.6
Total Single-Function Districts	29,036	31,821	2,785	9.6
MULTIFUNCTION DISTRICTS				
Natural Resources and Water Supply	131	102	–29	–22.1
Sewer and Water Supply	1,344	1,446	102	7.6
Other Multifunction Districts	1,044	1,627	583	55.8
Total Multifunction Districts	2,519	3,175	656	26.0
TOTAL	**31,555**	**34,996**	**3,441**	**10.9**

Sources: U.S. Census Bureau, *1992 Census of Governments, Government Organization*, Table 14; *2002 Census of Governments, Government Organization*, Table 9.

Although part of the increase in local government functions is attributable to state and federal mandates, at least part—and maybe most—is caused by increasing demands for more service by citizens. Part of the reason is that the nation is becoming increasingly complex economically, socially, and demographically. If everyone were similar in income, life-cycle stage, and general taste and preference priorities, only a limited range of services would be needed to meet their needs. For example, retirement communities do not usually need schools or ball fields, so they can do without them. A city composed of people of all ages and life-cycle stages needs to provide many diverse services.

Something else perhaps even more dramatic is occurring: the rise of "private government" in a highly decentralized fashion across the nation. Private government plays an increasingly larger role in defining the local regulatory and planning environments, especially in large Sunbelt metropolitan areas. Among our case analysis states, Arizona and Florida are particularly dominated by this form of local government (Lang and LeFurgy 2007). For instance, Weston, Florida, a town that is essentially one large master-planned community, has contracted out all its municipal services and maintains only three municipal employees—this in a city of 70,000 residents (Lang 2007). Similarly, many cities throughout Florida and Arizona, and to an increasing extent, Georgia and Virginia, have a significant share of residents living in private governments such as homeowners associations. The Community Association Institute—an Alexandria, Virginia–based trade group for HOAs—puts the figure nationwide at one in six Americans. It also finds that nearly half of new residential development (and virtually all new owner-occupied housing in Florida and Arizona) lies in HOAs. In addition to these HOAs are often business improvement districts (BIDs) that are used for everything from managing commercial areas to raising the money for major infrastructure such as highways.

The effect of private government is to mute differences between states in how they manage local planning and growth issues. An HOA in Arizona is pretty much the same as one in Florida in terms of how it enforces local codes or how it relates to traditional local public government. Lang and LeFurgy (2007) find that in many places, elected government is ceding local control to HOAs in an effort to reduce its burden of paying for infrastructure and managing neighborhood change. Municipalities are then freer to work on big issues, such as long-range planning and economic development. As a result, many local problems that might arise from disputes over property rights are now the domain of private government, where covenants contractually spell out rights and obligations. Indeed, local governments apparently are not only welcoming private governments—especially in the form of HOAs—but requiring them. A growing trend exists to condition approval of residential developments on the formation of HOAs; local governments are even specifying what HOA responsibilities are, how they function, and how they generate revenue.[11]

A growing trend also favors combining special districts with private governments. The most popular mode of melding the two appears to be through BIDs. Barely two decades old as an innovative governance device and then used only in New York City, BIDs have expanded in number, geography, and even scope (Houstoun, Levy, Gibson, and Kozloff 2003). BIDs are established through a voluntary agreement to create a private, nonprofit entity to tend to certain things of benefit to the members, such as street cleaning, beautification, marketing, and the like. BIDs also include a financial commitment. The financial obligation is typically implemented through locally enforced assessments that are passed through to the BID, but in return the BID makes annual reports to local government about how the funds were spent.

In recent years, the BID concept has grown to enhance the role of private government in serving as a pass-through mechanism for financing infrastructure. Use of HOAs and BIDS as a tool for funding local transportation and service improvements is now a common practice. In some instances, even major highway improvements—and even whole new highways, in some cases—may be paid for this way (Lang and LeFurgy 2007). For instance, big master-planned communities often use a bond that is charged to homeowners through a BID to pay for new ramps for freeways. This source of funding for costly infrastructure is universally available and is used often in the new pay-as-you-go climate for growth. As more places in the United States adopt this finance system, it should lead to even more convergence in how growth is managed.

Moving toward Common Ground

Five themes underlie an emerging dialogue that is common among states:
(a) adequate public facilities, (b) transportation, (c) open spaces and critical
landscapes, (d) affordable housing, and (e) economic development. In this
section, we highlight six states to illustrate that despite apparent differences
in political culture and location, they appear to be moving toward common
ground in certain respects.

Oregon

Among the contiguous 48 states, Oregon is arguably the one with the reputation
of being the most rigorous in growth management planning (Abbott, Adler, and
Howe 2003). Every city and urbanized area is contained within an urban growth
boundary; resource lands are restricted to nonresidential land uses unless such
uses are needed to sustain resource activities; cities and counties must meet housing targets, including affordable housing needs; and a top-down policy-making
and implementation system exists that gives the state the strongest role in overseeing local planning of any state other than perhaps Hawaii.

Oregon's planning system is composed of a Land Conservation and Development Commission (LCDC) that established overall statewide planning policies,
the Department of Land Conservation and Development that serves the LCDC,
the Land Use Board of Appeals that hears qualifying land use disputes in an
expedited format (it must render a decision within 120 days of appeal), and
cities and counties that must plan their jurisdictions and have plans approved
by the LCDC. Numerous ballot measures have attempted to terminate the program, but none has succeeded.

Nevertheless, numerous successful efforts have recognized a certain range of
property rights. In the early 1990s, recognizing that restrictive farming and forest
land use restrictions prevented individual owners from building homes on their
lots, the legislature passed HB 3661. This legislation was considered a safety valve
that solved perceived inequities among people who owned rural land before the
state planning process restricted their property to only resource uses.

In the 2000s, two efforts were launched to have the local government compensate landowners aggrieved by downzoning, especially in rural areas. Both measures passed, but the first, Ballot Measure 7, was ruled unconstitutional by the
state supreme court. The second, Ballot Measure 37, was ruled constitutional.[12]

It allows property owners to request compensation for their loss of property value attributable to a land use change during the time of their ownership or a waiver of the planning rules to allow them to develop based on the prior land use designations. Although some compensation has been given, many claims have resulted in local governments waiving the new rules and applying the old ones. Table 14 summarizes the claims made pursuant to Ballot Measure 37.

To prevent large-scale implementation of Ballot Measure 37, however, the Oregon legislature took the unusual step of putting an off-year measure on the November 2007 ballot, called Ballot Measure 49. As passed by the voters, it reduces the number of claims considerably, excludes nonresidential development from making Ballot Measure 37–based claims, and limits the number of qualifying residential permits to a range of three to ten, based on ownership history and availability of public facilities.[13]

Other lesser-known but no-less-important changes have been made to Oregon's system. Many of the procedural efficiencies advanced in Oregon have eroded over time. For instance, Oregon was a national leader in requiring fast-track permitting for developments meeting clear and objective land use criteria. Because plans have not kept pace with market changes, however, many existing plans need to be revised through lengthy public processes. More interesting is the Oregon courts' position that certain land use changes, especially annexations by cities of land outside their jurisdiction but inside the urban growth boundary and clearly anticipated to be annexed when market conditions warrant, may occur only after a favorable referendum by city voters. Thus, what was planned locally and approved by the state may not happen if voters reject the annexation.

Finally, despite Oregon's planning innovations, it does not have a transfer of development rights program that may allow developers to buy development rights to resource land ("sending areas") to use inside urban growth boundaries ("receiving areas").

On the whole, Oregon's planning system seems to be becoming more sensitive than in the past to property rights of individuals caught in changing land use designations.

Table 14. Oregon Ballot Measure 37 Claims as of May 25, 2007

6,749—Measure 37 claims received.

3,044—Claims closed (final order or withdrawal).

3,565—Claims remaining.

3,113—Claims with "neighbor letters" sent, totaling 61,257 letters.

$19 billion-plus—Total compensation requested.

Source: Summarized from Oregon Department of Land Conservation and Development Web site, www.oregon.gov/LCD/MEASURE37/summaries_of_claims.shtml#Summaries_of_Claims_Filed_in_the_State (accessed July 28, 2007).

Florida

Florida's modern planning epoch began at about the same time as Oregon's with the passage of legislation in the early and mid-1970s that required state involvement in Areas of Critical State Concern and Developments of Regional Impact, and required local governments to prepare comprehensive plans. Not until the landmark Growth Management Act of 1985, however, did planning become entrenched in the state. Borrowing from Oregon, this act included implied (but did not mandate) urban containment measures, affordable housing obligations, preservation of resource lands, and so forth. As in Oregon, local governments were required to prepare plans consistent with a State Comprehensive Plan (FS 186). The state Department of Community Affairs wrote and implemented the planning rules; reviewed plans for their consistency with state planning policy; and advanced such pioneering planning concepts as "concurrency," whereby development is not allowed unless facilities needed to serve it are in place or planned to be in place "concurrent with the impacts of development."

Like Oregon, Florida had an overall policy-making body, but in its case composed of the governor and cabinet (who are statewide elected officials), and a special land use adjudication process (the Division of Administrative Hearings within the state Department of Justice). Finally, as in Oregon, the principal champion of statewide land use planning was a Republican governor—in Oregon, Tom McCall, and in Florida, Bob Martinez.

Unlike Oregon, Florida does not have a citizen-driven initiative process so citizens have no opportunity to vote on statewide planning efforts. Concerns about Florida's planning are thus dealt with almost exclusively by the legislature, but the governor also has considerable influence. As originally designed, Florida's legislation includes extensive public participation requirements as part of various planning processes. For instance, two hearings are required of every comprehensive plan amendment, and affected parties have opportunities to challenge any planning decisions in the state's Division of Administrative Hearings, which can process land use cases more quickly than cases brought to other courts.

Over the past dozen years or so, Florida's land use planning pendulum has swung toward more flexibility and recognition of certain property rights based on thresholds. In the mid-1990s, concurrency standards for transportation were relaxed somewhat so that congestion of roads need not prevent further urban development (Chapin 2007). In 1995, the Bert Harris Act allowed property owners to seek compensation for loss of property values if land use changes reduced value by more than 40 percent. This provision has been exercised in court several times, but often claims are settled between local governments and property owners. In addition, in recent years the ability of interest groups to challenge local land use decisions has been curtailed while the state has facilitated expedited land use decision making under certain circumstances, often without the due diligence that is accorded other development prospects. One important practical effect is that downzonings of land—no matter how sensible—are discouraged because compensation may be owed.

Georgia

In 1989, Georgia became the second southern state to mandate comprehensive planning consistent with state goals and review by a state agency. (Florida was the first state in the middle 1980s.) Every county and city was required to prepare comprehensive plans meeting state goals relating to population and housing, economic development, facilities and services, environmental protection, and coordination. All jurisdictions came into compliance by the middle 1990s. Unlike in Florida and Oregon, however, standards for meeting state goals were modest, and for the most part, sophisticated jurisdictions already had plans exceeding the "minimum planning standards" adopted by the state.

Yet the past decade has seen considerable change in Georgia's planning landscape. In 1996, every county and its constituent jurisdictions were to have adopted a plan to coordinate the provision, management, and financing of all public facilities within the county. In 2000, on the heels of the state violating federal ambient air quality standards, the Georgia Regional Transportation Authority was created and applied to the 13 counties composing the most urbanized portion of the Atlanta metropolitan area. The Georgia Community

Greenspace Program mentioned earlier was adopted in 2001, and to address regional waters issues in northern Georgia, the Metropolitan North Georgia Water District was formed in 2002. By 2005, the minimum planning standards had been revised, creating three classes of planning for (a) rural/slow-growing, (b) smaller and moderately growing, and (c) large (more than 50,000 population) and/or rapidly growing counties. Each class has to meet different levels of requirements to continue its "qualified local government" status (and thus remain eligible for state funds). The most rigorous category sets standards coming close to the expectations of Florida and Oregon.

Wisconsin

No two states have identical planning environments or legislation. Political and planning traditions, government structures, and social and environmental factors as well as population and economic pressures all play roles in the creation and implementation of a state's planning legislation. Wisconsin offers relevance to this report because of the diversity of the state itself. States that have enacted planning reforms lie predominantly on the East and West Coasts, such as California, Oregon, and Florida, where growth has occurred at a faster rate than in the geographic center. Planning legislation in faster-growing regions may not seem applicable to states in the heartland, yet these are the places where metropolitan land consumption per new resident is very high.

Various laws in the past few years, such as those related to large-scale livestock siting, nonmetallic mining, stormwater management, and wetland protection, have given the state an increasingly larger role in local planning. The state's influence in planning issues has perhaps never been greater perhaps because of these particular state-level interests.

Wisconsin faces some of the same issues as many other more rural, midcountry states, yet it also faces issues similar to states on the East and West Coasts. In addition, as a state bordering the Great Lakes, Wisconsin is considered by the federal government as a coastal state, partaking in many of the same federal coastal management and planning programs as states of the East and West Coasts.

An economic boom in the 1980s and early 1990s led to demographic shifts as well as suburban development that, while modest compared to the faster-growing parts of the country, was nonetheless a milestone after previous decades of slow growth. Wisconsin has also recently lost manufacturing jobs and experienced a population shift away from many of its cities. Not unlike many other states, Wisconsin has both a rural and an urban culture and embraces strong local control tendencies. Local comprehensive planning experiences detail how some of the prominent issues regarding land use planning are playing out within a new framework for local planning.

In the mid-1990s, a diverse group of advocates crafted new guidelines for local comprehensive planning.[14] The Wisconsin legislature passed the legislation known as Act 9 in 1999. It includes five elements:[15]

■ Beginning on January 1, 2010, zoning, subdivision, and official mapping ordinances must be consistent with the local government's comprehensive plan (not all local governments have zoning, subdivision, and official mapping ordinances, so not every local government will need to have a comprehensive plan).

■ Public participation and intergovernmental coordination are required.

■ A comprehensive plan—for which the legislation provides the state's first definition—must address the following nine elements: issues and opportunities; housing; transportation; utilities and community facilities; agricultural, natural, and cultural resources; economic development; intergovernmental cooperation; land use; and implementation.

■ State Comprehensive Planning Grant funds are available to support planning, and as of June 2007, they have been used by more than 900 communities (almost half of the local governments in the state).

■ Cities and villages with more than 12,500 residents must enact a traditional neighborhood development (TND) ordinance.[16]

Wisconsin jurisdictions have through the end of the decade to prepare plans consistent with these guidelines.

Other factors are at work. Since 1989, the Nelson-Knowles Stewardship Fund has made $60 million available per year for land preservation acquisition efforts. In part for this reason, roughly 20 percent of the state is in public ownership.[17] The governor has proposed increasing funding to $105 million per year. The state Department of Natural Resources oversees this program along with the State Conservation and Outdoor Recreation Plan. This program represents a substantial state-level commitment to targeted open-space preservation.

Beyond financing, Wisconsin has had a shoreland zoning program from the 1960s; this law got Wisconsin included as one of the original "quiet revolution" states. This program, along with state-mandated floodplain zoning, illustrates Wisconsin's reliance on zoning to protect open space and natural landscapes, much like Florida and Oregon. Given the number of lakes and rivers in Wisconsin, these programs have had important influence on shaping development patterns.

Virginia

Planning in Virginia is based on authority through the "Dillon rule" doctrine rather than the "home rule" doctrine that every other state reviewed for this report follows, with some exceptions in Wisconsin.[18] Under the Dillon rule doctrine, local governments are creatures of the state, subordinate to the state legislature. Counties, cities, and regional governmental organizations (such as planning districts and metropolitan planning organizations) can exercise control over growth and development *only* through those authorities specifically identified by the legislature. Indeed, in theory and often in practice, some jurisdictions may be granted planning authorities and others none. Still, all jurisdictions in Virginia have planning and zoning enabling authority.

Virginia local governments enjoy planning powers comparable to, if not sometimes in excess of, those of other leading states. For example, while Oregon may require urban growth boundaries around all its urban areas, Virginia enables the same requirement. As a result, the outlying counties of the heavily urbanized northern Virginia region as well as parts of the Tidewater region and selected other jurisdictions (such as Albemarle County where the University of Virginia is located) have comparable urban development limits. Indeed, perhaps because of this requirement, new net residential densities in northern Virginia are as high as or higher than those in other suburban regions of "growth managed" states.

Virginia also has three regional transportation authorities with jurisdictions covering the heavily populated northern Virginia region, which is where about half of metropolitan Washington, D.C.'s suburban residents live. Indeed, the northern Virginia suburbs may have more transportation options in the journey to work than do comparable regions outside New York City and Chicago.

In the arena of open space and environmental protection, although the state does not have a dedicated fund for conservation land acquisition, Virginia's legislature annually appropriates up to $100 million to provide tax credits to facilitate the donation of conservation easements on open-space land, making it a national leader in easement donation. In addition, most of the state's population is managed under the federal and state Chesapeake Bay acts.

In 2006, the Virginia legislature expanded much of the state's planning laws. For jurisdictions over 20,000 in population or those growing at about the national average each decade, important new powers were granted, including the ability to attach conditions to rezoning approval,[19] enact road impact fees, and allow the transfer of development rights.

Despite apparently limited planning authority, growth management–style planning is not only possible in Virginia but has already been recognized with national awards. Arlington County has been cited by the U.S. Environmental Protection Agency and the Urban Land Institute for its "smart growth" planning.

Arizona

Arizona is an interesting case with a split personality in terms of progressive planning. As the land of conservative Barry Goldwater, the state has a strong libertarian tradition and a general distrust of government intrusion in personal affairs such as property rights. Yet a vivid sense also exists that Arizona's desert lands are fragile and need protecting. Collective action on water use is also needed, which serves to dampen the go-it-alone ethos of the West.

Arizona has benefited from having current and recent governors from both parties with good environmental records. In 1980, Democratic governor Bruce Babbitt began this trend by negotiating and steering the passage of the 1980 Groundwater Management Act. This act gave the state the most comprehensive water regulatory system in the nation. Even Babbitt recognized, however, that "Effective land use and water management laws are not about slowing economic growth or discouraging people from coming to Arizona. To the contrary, good planning will protect and preserve the values that continue to attract people and growth."[20] Babbitt was also responsible for creation of the Arizona Department of Water Resources and the Arizona Department of Environmental Quality and a major expansion of the state park system. Much of Arizona's modern planning culture is shaped by these insights from a generation ago.

In 1996, the Arizona legislature passed the Arizona Preserve Initiative in an attempt to encourage preservation of select parcels of state trust land in and around urban areas. A 1998 amendment provided a $220 million public/private matching grant program to assist in the purchase or lease of state trust lands for conservation. The Arizona State Land Department has indefinitely suspended this effort because of concerns raised by program opponents who argue that the program is unconstitutional because it does not guarantee that state trust lands will be sold for their highest and best use.

Also in 1998, the local chapter of the Sierra Club started a petition drive to put on the ballot a comprehensive growth management initiative. Although it was unsuccessful in putting the initiative on the ballot, pro-development forces joined with Republican governor Jane Hull to lobby the state legislature to pass "Growing Smarter"—legislation that required cities to adopt general plans that incorporate open-space preservation, growth management, environmental planning, and impact fees. This law required better planning for open spaces and provided $20 million a year for 11 years for the state to purchase open space in urban areas. Growing Smarter contained no penalties for jurisdictions that failed to produce plans.

Governor Hull also supported follow-up measures to strengthen Growing Smarter. These proposals required communities to write and follow general plans that address important issues such as transportation and gave counties more authority to fight poorly planned "wildcat" subdivisions. Growing Smarter Plus was passed in 2000; it required cities and counties to submit plans to voters for approval and authorized (but did not require) a fund to purchase development rights from private owners. Growing Smarter Plus deflected attention from an aggressive growth management initiative on the November 2000 ballot, which ultimately was defeated.

The current governor, Janet Napolitano, recently assembled a "growth cabinet" that is charged with creating a comprehensive set of proposals to address the issue of sustainable development. Napolitano intends to make growth the signature issue for her second term. Some of the preliminary ideas floated by the growth cabinet include a high-speed rail line between Phoenix and Tucson.

Despite a history of progressive governors, Arizonans are still responsive to politics that promise to protect private interests from government intrusion. Witness the passage of Proposition 207 in 2006, which was a recent reaction to negative publicity associated with the *Kelo v. New London* case, fueled by a well-publicized 2001 local case in which the city of Mesa (a large suburb of Phoenix) initiated eminent domain action against a longtime downtown business, Bailey's Brake Shop, to replace it with an Ace Hardware. Proposition 207 is an eminent domain reform packaged with a regulatory takings measure (borrowing language from Oregon's Measure 207). The new rules make taking private property for the purposes of redevelopment much harder, and they also broadly define takings to include any downzoning that will affect property value.

Proposition 207 has had several consequences for Arizona land use regulation. First, it has slowed down cities attempting comprehensive revision of their zoning ordinances. Second, it has added new layers of legal and planning review to consider Proposition 207 implications. For example, places such as Scottsdale, which use overlay districts in some older neighborhoods to prevent the spread of "McMansions," now face the prospect of abandoning this strategy or incurring stiff costs for private takings claims. The bottom line is that Arizona is on a complicated course where it has lost key tools to manage growth at the local level, but it will soon have a new set of state policies that seek to create more sustainable growth.

Common Ground

Among the six states reviewed, all face growth pressures in their metropolitan areas, if not statewide. Several states, including Florida, Georgia, Oregon, and Wisconsin, require that all local governments establish level of service (LOS) delivery standards for key facilities, and Virginia requires LOS standards for roads for jurisdictions of a certain size and growth rate. To facilitate provision of adequate public facilities, all states, including Arizona, allow impact fees through enabling legislation or home rule authority. All impact fee programs require formal adoption of LOS delivery standards (such as improved acres of parkland per 1,000 residents). All states also enable, and some mandate, comprehensive planning that includes establishing LOS standards, projecting facility needs, and crafting financing plans to meet those needs. Most states provide some state-level financing of schools and roads, and most also provide low-interest loans for utilities. All states allow local governments to consider facility capacity to accommodate the demands of new development on "discretionary" land use approvals such as rezonings and subdivisions.[21] Only Oregon, however, requires that sufficient land be designated for projected development in planning and zoning ordinances throughout the jurisdiction—and be served or planned to be served with adequate public facilities, thus reducing considerably public opposition to new development based on that argument. Nonetheless, all states face tens of billions of dollars in unfunded demands for new, expanded, or replaced facilities to accommodate development over the next generation.

In most states, financing transportation improvements is the single largest unfunded demand.[22] All states have unique state/local transportation financing and management arrangements. Virginia, for example, assumes management of local subdivision streets if they meet state construction standards—with the result that jurisdictions in nearly all growing areas of the state require that subdivisions install streets meeting state standards, thereby ensuring that the long-range maintenance and repair costs are shifted to the state. In contrast, Oregon requires local governments to develop plans that will reduce dependency on the single-occupant vehicle by about 20 percent by 2020 and provides some state funding to invest in alternative transportation modes. On a miles per million residents basis, Florida is the largest state with the smallest rail transit network while Georgia is the largest state without state-level funding of local transit systems.[23] Arizona and Wisconsin have traditional state highway programs that do not address public transit significantly, although the Phoenix metropolitan area is funding an aggressive light-rail system through a combination of local taxes and revenues, federal funds, and some state funds.

The bottom line, however, is that transportation funding is at best a mixed bag and at worst a hindrance to achieving efficient land use patterns—and even a hindrance to sustaining economic development. One of the problems may be the structure and operation of metropolitan planning organizations (MPOs). MPOs exist for every metropolitan region of the nation and are the official conduits of federal funds for transportation investments. The planning and policy-making responsibilities rest with nonelected boards, appointed to their positions by elected city and county governing bodies. These boards have final say on how federal funds are used and are thus the primary decision-making body for metropolitan-scale transportation planning. The problem is that, for the most part, MPOs are skewed toward representing suburban interests and invest more in transportation systems that expand suburban development than in integrating metropolitan areas through alternative transportation modes (Nelson, Sanchez, and Wolf 2004). Neither the states nor the federal government seems interested in or willing to alter the representational structure of MPOs. Moreover, as metropolitan areas begin to merge with each other, neither the states nor the federal government seems prepared to alter the role of MPOs to consider "megapolitan" implications of transportation demands (see Lang and Nelson 2007).

Preservation of open spaces and critical landscapes is considered a priority in all six states, but each approaches the concern very differently. Oregon and Florida rely heavily on land use planning and zoning to preserve such landscapes (through mandatory elements subject to state oversight), but Florida goes one step further by having perhaps the nation's most aggressive state-level effort to acquire such lands. Development pressures combined with the public's concern about sensitive landscapes have likely created a willingness to raise taxes to acquire land. Oregon may not be as concerned at the state level because more than half the state is owned by the federal government and another quarter is owned by the state.

Arizona does not have a strong state-level planning mandate to preserve certain landscapes, but, like Oregon, more than three-quarters of the state is publicly owned while another sizable percentage is tribal lands. Indeed, Arizona has a slightly different problem in that vast public landownership inhibits efficient development where it is needed most. Gammage (1999) reviews how state agencies work with development interests to facilitate the interests of each. Generally, the state land department sells or leases land it determines is not needed for state purposes at auction to the highest bidder. Often, the land released for bid by the state is that which is substantially surrounded or affected by urban development. The overall result is development often contiguous to existing development. The state also buys land from private interests if that land advances certain state interests.

The other three states have no state-level oversight of local planning to preserve open space and critical landscapes, nor a substantial state-level commitment to acquire such lands, nor large volumes of publicly owned land. Yet they have aggressive preservation efforts. Georgia is on a pace to spend more than a half billion dollars between 2002 and 2020 to acquire "greenspaces," and local efforts seem to at least double the leverage. Virginia relies on private landowner donations of development rights (through conservation easements) that are facilitated by the nation's most aggressive use of state tax credits—about $100 million annually. Wisconsin has had the Stewardship Fund since 1989, which has been funded at $60 million annually since 1999 and is proposed to increase to $105 million per year. Wisconsin has had a state shoreland zoning program since the 1960s and a state-level program mandating zoning protection of floodplains.

Although superficially a priority among all six states, affordable housing is a mixed bag. All states take advantage of the Treasury Department's low- and moderate-income housing tax credit programs, but Georgia requires only the minimum 15-year commitment period to rent the subsidized units to target households—which means that Georgia is now merely replacing units constructed 15 years ago with newly subsidized units. All other states require at least 30-year commitment contracts. Florida probably has the most aggressive state-level subsidy effort and also expedites local permitting of affordable housing land use proposals. Oregon requires all local governments to identify low- and moderate-income housing needs and to plan and zone land to meet those needs. It also has an expedited permitting process, but the legislature has removed inclusionary housing requirements as a condition of locally approved projects. None of the other states has significant affordable housing efforts, and no state monitors local production of affordable housing against state-level targets for the purpose of prospective sanctions.

Likewise, all states make economic development a priority but again through different planning approaches. All states have tax-based incentive programs to encourage new job formation that differ only in nuance. Some states will go to extraordinary efforts to lure economic development. Florida pledged a half billion dollars to facilitate a new research facility in the agricultural preserve of Palm Beach County for the Scripps Research Institute and expedited review processes allowing it to locate on a site surrounded by agricultural land and requiring workers to drive many miles from urban centers to reach it. Although the site was approved by the state and survived court challenges, Scripps ultimately decided to locate the facility in an area known as Jupiter located inside the urban area—right where interest groups opposing the original location had recommended.[24] Oregon's "silicon forest" (an area west of downtown Portland where several world headquarters of high-tech firms are located) owes its success to a decision in the 1980s that redirected prime farmland for this purpose. These are only anecdotes illustrating the lengths to which states may go to lure marquee economic development that may otherwise be inconsistent with certain state planning goals.

By and large, we find convergence of the states on addressing key issues such as those noted here. Although the state-level policies may vary, the outcomes may be more similar than the approaches are different.

Synthesizing Perspectives

This report was informed by many people, including a panel engaged twice—first to assess the state of state-level planning broadly, and second to assess the report's final version. This section synthesizes initial perspectives offered by the panel and elaborates on the themes it presented.

Getting beyond the Debate on "Whether to Plan"

In many states, the debate on "whether to plan" has been settled. Over the next generation, planning advanced at the state level and implemented locally (often through state/regional/local planning collaborations) will be crucial in managing investment of trillions of dollars in taxpayer money (Nelson 2006). Highways, utilities, schools, drainage, and transit are especially big-ticket public investments that can shape land use patterns. If development does not go where those investments are made, inefficiencies, such as higher taxes and utility rates, are likely to occur and perhaps dampen economic development. For these and related reasons, many states have advanced local planning to address state-level interests and, although we might quibble about the form and effectiveness of those efforts, they have come a long way in a short time. State-level interest in local planning is now embedded in the land use process in many states, even those not deemed "smart growth."

Second, many states are moving away from regulations to encouraging if not requiring local governments to measure and assess outcomes. Florida is beginning the process of reconsidering its onerous planning requirements and slimming down the regulatory requirements in an effort to get local governments to focus more on development outcomes (such as density, design, and mixed use). Georgia has retooled its entire statewide planning system to expect more from larger, growing jurisdictions than in the past. Virginia continues to give local governments more financial and land use planning powers despite its reputation as a Dillon rule state.

Third, an emerging interest exists in design as a part of the planning process. States are starting to realize that design standards matter and that encouraging and enabling local governments to consider design during the land use planning process is useful. Both Florida and Georgia require special review of "developments of regional impact" that focuses increasingly more on design issues than on the actual volume and distribution of development. Wisconsin requires every jurisdiction to adopt and implement a traditional neighborhood development option including statutory language expecting its widespread use.

Fourth, concerns about effects on private property owners have also become part of the mainstream discussion on the role of the state in advancing local planning. This concern is not so much a retrenchment of state-level planning interests as a recognition that as new systems are created to advance state and local interests new ways of addressing effects on property rights also need to be created.

Finally, an ongoing tension remains in many states between the need to manage growth in urbanizing areas and to promote growth in economically stagnant rural areas. It is a major issue in all the states reviewed in this report plus many others—such as Maryland, New Jersey, Tennessee, Utah, and Washington, to name just a few.

In every case we reviewed and in others, we find that state-level planning systems—especially those one may classify as "growth management systems"—are tailored to individual state's particular objectives, legal structure, and political culture (see also Porter 2007). States are moving away from a one-size-fits-all growth management model to one that is more responsive. It is on this last point that much of the rest of this section is predicated.

Do Not Just Look at Interstate Divides on This Issue; Focus Also on Intrastate Splits

The panel observed that in state planning, one size does not fit all—yet for some of the most notable examples of state planning, every local government was required to meet one-size-fits-all rules, especially in Florida, Georgia, and Oregon. The "new dialogue" recognizes the shortcomings of this one-size-fits-all approach. Georgia was the first to create clear differences in level of expectations of local governments based on their size, location, and growth rate. The new governor of Florida, Charlie Crist, installed a new secretary of the Department of Community Affairs who intends to reshape planning rules to be similarly sympathetic to differences among Florida jurisdictions. Virginia's planning has long differentiated between jurisdictions based on their size, location, and growth rates.

The divide in how localities interpret state planning initiatives is also partly determined by whether the locality is within a megapolitan area. The challenges of megapolitan area development, all of which will have at least 5 million residents by 2040, means that cooperative action is needed in areas such as transportation investment and environmental protection. Panelists noted that places swept up in large-scale, concentrated development seemed more willing to seek state-level solutions to manage growth.

For instance, a split exists between northern Virginia (NOVA), which is part of the booming Washington, D.C., metropolitan area, and the rest of Virginia (ROVA) in terms of the local politics of planning. Consider issues such as transportation, where ROVA resists funding projects in NOVA. In terms of land use planning, NOVA seems to be converging with the D.C. metropolitan area. Here, a much greater interest exists in land preservation and smart growth practices than in ROVA. A big part of this support is caused by the rapidly shifting politics of NOVA. Two decades back, only small sections of Alexandria and Arlington were concerned with what are now called smart growth policies. Now, all the area inside the Washington, D.C., beltway appears to be so inclined, as is much of Fairfax County (the state's most populous county) along with a growing number of exurban counties. This shift was noticeable even comparing the 2000 and 2004 presidential vote. In the 2005 governor's race and the 2006 U.S. Senate midterm election, Democratic candidates won Fairfax by wide margins and even managed to win exurban Loudoun and Prince William counties by slim margins.

The trend should continue, and the much faster growth in the progressive— planning-friendly—parts of Virginia means that state planning efforts should be better received in the future. Our observation is based on its divided politics. Virginia's divided politics are not unique. An upstate (Atlanta)/downstate split in Georgia, a contrast between the urban Sun Corridor (or Phoenix and Tucson) and rural parts of Arizona, and a divisive dynamic between the Willamette Valley and the rest of Oregon were visible in the latest wave of statewide referenda on eminent domain and regulatory takings. For example, Measure 7, a regulatory takings proposition that overturned Oregon's land use planning, received more support from rural areas than from urban ones. In Arizona, a combined regulatory takings/eminent domain proposition passed with strong support in the exurbs and rural areas. The same was true for a Georgia law limiting eminent domain.

The state divides identified by the panelists affect multiple planning issues, including property rights, environmental policy, land use regulation, transportation investment, and energy and climate change efforts. In all places, the more urban and built up an area is, the more likely it is to support broad planning powers at the state level. By contrast, the metropolitan fringe and rural areas are more likely to limit those efforts. Part of the convergence in state policy reflects the compromises the internal divides within the states are producing that result in a middle course of planning action. Most states with large-scale urbanization or a history of progressive rural politics (such as Vermont) will support at least some modest statewide planning goals.

States with referenda that limit planning action—as in the case of Proposition 207 in Arizona—may limit some key tools needed to redevelop cities. In this case, a state law has a targeted impact and will most affect places that seek the powers of eminent domain to remake urban space. In instances where a new regulatory takings referendum passed, the ability to downzone areas may now constitute a taking. Thus, the preservation of neighborhood context in areas where greater intensity of land use is occurring may now trigger a takings charge by owners seeking, for instance, to build a large home on a small lot.

Who Pays for Infrastructure?

The panel addressed the issue of infrastructure financing. It is interesting to note that every state reviewed in this report uses impact fees either through explicit enabling legislation or based on decades of case-law guidance (such as Florida); even Virginia, with its Dillon rule doctrine, enables impact fee–like "proffers" in all the urbanized and rapidly growing jurisdictions.

An underlying concern in these and other states is a free-rider problem in that development in some communities may not pay the true cost for infrastructure. In the past, newer developing areas could count on a subsidy from already built-up places for a large share of infrastructure costs. Now, the trend is that development outside demarcated service boundaries needs to shoulder a bigger share of infrastructure costs. State planning efforts have played a role in this shift to better cost accounting by designating areas that have existing services and offering incentives for staying within those boundaries and disincentives for developing outside those areas. A new trend, begun in places such as Las Vegas, is to adopt private governance models—for example, business improvement districts—as revenue generators to pay the costs of infrastructure in rapidly developing areas.

What Role Do Innovative Developers Play?

According to the panel, the diffusing of new development practices by large builders effectively mutes some of the differences in planning efforts between states and fits with our convergence model. Consider how the recent innovation of infill development in and around Atlanta has changed that region's and the state of Georgia's perception on community development. Just two decades back, denser, mixed-use development was virtually unknown in Atlanta. Now the region has numerous cases where mixed-use projects serve as national case studies. The panel argued that these developer-led efforts to remake urban and older suburban space have changed the conversation at the state level. Rather than argue for mixed-use projects to fulfill abstract goals such as reducing sprawl, planners can show politicians from across Georgia examples where alternative planning practices are working.

How You Act Depends on Where You Sit

All elected officials do not see state planning efforts in the same way. For example, mayors of big cities—even big suburban cities—commonly want more tools to manage growth. Interestingly, this pattern cuts across party lines. Mayors want more regulatory options because they have to manage multiple externalities at the local level. In short, they need all the tools they can have to manage neighborhood change. In contrast, state legislators, who are often much further removed from tackling local problems, have the luxury of playing politics with issues such as property rights. Thus the property rights movement receives little support from elected officials managing large municipalities, including many Republican mayors who may even express an ideological concern that the state not impinge on the rights of property owners. Yet Republicans in the state legislature with a similar libertarian bent can stoke the property rights issue as a way to gain reelection.

A New Dialogue Is Emerging

The panelists argued that a new dialogue has emerged around state planning issues. The new dialogue also implies that the debate has moved on from old positions that time has rendered less relevant. Part of this shift, ironically, is caused by the declining influence of councils of governments and regional planning efforts. States are partly filling this void and are working out compromises with and between localities. The solutions are less focused on grand plans and edicts issued from the state and instead concern practical solutions that involve multiple stakeholders.

The emergence of new markets for alternative products to conventional development and the rise of builders seeking to meet this demand have removed much of the stigma from denser and mixed-use projects. In the past, planners framed alternative development as a necessary medicine needed to fix the ills of the metropolis. In this new dialogue, alternatives to convention are now seen in terms of opportunity—even as engines of economic development.

Recent elections indicate that the public also seems much more open to new environmental and transportation solutions. Consider the amount of open-space legislation that has recently passed statewide votes. At the metropolitan level, regions long dominated by cars have overwhelmingly voted for light-rail systems. Some places, such as Salt Lake City, are even on their second round of rail initiatives, having approved a $2.5 billion expansion of the existing system that includes 40 new stations. In fact, rail will now link the entire Wasatch Front, which accounts for over 80 percent of Utah's population.

We are clearly in an interesting time for state planning. From one perspective, the public seems eager to limit planning power by passing new property rights referenda. Yet the same public is willing to preserve land, pay for new transit alternatives, and live in more urban settings. The mood is one that mixes a concern about fairness and rights with an approach more open to exploring alternative development solutions. This new dialogue is not limited to Red or Blue states but seems to cut in complicated ways within states. It may be driven by a growing sense among metropolitan residents especially that the way we grow now is broken, which translates into an increasing openness to alternative practices.

Notes

1. We are indebted to Deborah Howe for coining the term "new dialogue" that best characterizes our view of the state of land use controls that has emerged in this century.

2. *Village of Euclid v. Ambler Realty Co.*, 272 U.S. 365, 395 (1926), where the Court held that a zoning ordinance would be unconstitutional if it is "clearly arbitrary and unreasonable" and thus has "no substantial relation to the public health, safety, morals, or general welfare."

3. *Nectow v. City of Cambridge*, 277 U.S. 183, 188–89 (1928), where the Court found that a zoning ordinance would be held unconstitutional under the 14th Amendment if it deprived the plaintiff of his property without due process of law—as was determined in this case.

4. *Pennsylvania Coal Co. v. Mahon*, 260 U.S. 393, 415 (1922), which provided that although property may be regulated to a certain extent, if regulation goes too far, it will be recognized as a taking—hence, become a "regulatory" taking as opposed to a physical one.

5. *Kelo v. City of New London*, 545 U.S. 469 (2005).

6. Some measures are initiatives put on the ballot if a certain number of voters sign petitions supporting a vote, while other measures are referenda placed on the ballot by legislatures.

7. Arthur C. Nelson and Robert E. Lang, adapted from U.S. Bureau of the Census, *2008 Statistical Abstract of the United States*, www.census.gov/prod/2007pubs/08statab/geo.pdf (accessed August 7, 2008).

8. From www.nps.gov/ncrc/programs/lwcf/ (accessed June 3, 2007).

9. Resources for the Land and Water Conservation Fund have not increased since its inception. Its funding peaked in the late 1970s; then after two decades of faltering and stagnant funding, it has spiked again. But under the second Bush administration, LWCF funding goes to federal agencies or to "other purposes," especially voluntary private conservation efforts that may not be conservation per se.

10. A handful of publicly operated land trusts and public/private partnerships are not reviewed here (see Mason, 2007).

11. This insight is from a symposium on regulatory barriers to affordable housing convened by the U.S. Department of Housing and Urban Development in Washington, D.C., June 15, 2007.

12. The Oregon Supreme Court ruled on narrow grounds that Ballot Measure 7 did not qualify as a constitutional amendment. Ballot Measure 37 was statutory in nature and not a constitutional amendment.

13. Polls indicate this measure is favored by a two-to-one margin, but as a predictor of special elections in an off year, such polls have considerable room for error.

14. This process was facilitated by a member of the review panel used to develop this report: Brian Ohm.

15. The legislation also included a smart growth dividend aid program that would have provided state aid to local governments that encouraged compact development and affordable housing. The program, however, was never funded. This program is part of the reason the law was originally referred to as the "smart growth" law (Ohm 2000). See also Ohm 2005.

16. Wisconsin also has towns, another general-purpose form of government, that govern the unincorporated areas. Towns do not have to adopt TND ordinances even though they are some of the fastest-growing communities in the state. The deadline for the TND requirement was in 2001; it is separate from the 2010 comprehensive planning requirement.

17. Information accessed July 15, 2007, from http://dnr.wi.gov/org/caer/cfa/lr/stewardship/stewardship.html.

18. Wisconsin has more than 1,200 towns that can plan, but they do not have home rule. Counties in Wisconsin have administrative home rule only, although they have flexibility in how they organize themselves administratively. Although cities and villages have home rule, it is seldom used. Especially in planning and zoning matters, cities and villages are creatures of the state and need get their authority from and follow the enabling laws.

19. Virginia is famous in land use planning and development law circles for having developers "voluntarily" proffer concessions if the local government approves a proposed rezoning. Oddly, although the proffer system was intended to keep local governments from imposing excessive exaction demands, quite the opposite happened. Voluntary concessions are viewed much differently in the courts from exactions conditioned on rezonings, which must abide by "essential nexus" and "rough proportionality" judicial standards.

20. Quoted in the *Arizona Republic*, May 2, 2004.

21. School capacity cannot be considered in Oregon, but the capacity of other facilities may be.

22. Florida provides substantial funding for new schools that is often matched with locally generated taxes and impact fees. All other states provide some level of state support for local school construction. All states have statutes enabling local water, wastewater, and stormwater utilities to finance expansion needs through revenue bonds, tap-on fees, and the like, essentially ensuring complete financing of those facilities. In our view, transportation financing creates the single largest unfunded financing demand among all facilities usually provided by local government.

23. The Georgia Regional Transportation Authority was established in 2000 in part to address public transit needs in the 13-county air quality nonattainment area in and surrounding Atlanta. Although technically a state agency, its jurisdiction is limited, and it essentially must self-finance public transit investments through revenue bonds, federal subsidies, and fare-box revenue and even by requiring local governments to finance a share of transit expenses through the local general fund.

24. Palm Beach County actually acquired the site Scripps wanted originally and began preparing it for development before Scripps selected a site inside the urban area. The county now owns a site surrounded by farms, miles away from urban infrastructure with tens of millions invested in acquisition and site preparation. The authors view this case study as a lesson in due diligence because alternative feasible sites existed with urban facilities and services that were much closer to the workforce.

Acknowledgments

The authors acknowledge the contribution of several leaders in the fields of state, regional, and local planning, some of whose assistance to the project was extraordinary. They include, in alphabetical order:

Tim Chapin
Associate Professor
University of Florida

Grady Gammage
Fellow, Morrison Institute
Arizona State University

Patricia Gober
Associate Professor
Arizona State University

Deborah Howe
Director, Urban Affairs and Planning
Temple University

William H. Hudnut
Senior Resident Fellow
ULI/Joseph C. Canizaro Chair for
    Public Policy
Urban Land Institute

Gerrit J. Knaap
Director, National Smart Growth
    Center
University of Maryland

Shelly Mastran
Professor in Practice
Virginia Tech

Brian W. Ohm
Head, Urban Affairs and Planning
University of Wisconsin

Douglas R. Porter
President
Growth Management Institute

Frederick R. Steiner
Dean, College of Architecture
University of Texas at Austin

Jerry Weitz
Editor, *Practicing Planner*
President, Weitz & Associates

References

Abbott, C., S. Adler, and D.A. Howe. 2003. A quiet counterrevolution in land use control: The origins and impacts of Oregon's Measure 7. *Housing Policy Debate* 14(3): 383–425.

Bosselman, Fred, and David Callies. 1971. *The Quiet Revolution in Land Use Control.* Washington, D.C.: Government Printing Office.

Chapin, Timothy S. 2007. Local governments as policy entrepreneurs: Evaluating Florida's "Concurrency Experiment." *Urban Affairs Review* 42(4): 505–32.

Chapin, Timothy S., and John V. Thomas. 2007. Assessing the Community Development District (CDD) model of infrastructure financing. Florida State University, Department of Urban and Regional Planning, Faculty Working Paper #07-04. www.fsu.edu/~durp/pdf_files/WPS_07-04_Chapin.pdf (accessed July 15, 2007).

DeGrove, John M. 1984. *Land, Growth and Politics.* Chicago: American Planning Association.

———. 2005. *Planning Policy and Politics: Smart Growth and the States.* Cambridge, Mass.: Lincoln Institute for Land Policy.

DeGrove, John M., and Deborah Miness. 1992. *The New Frontier for Land Policy: Planning and Growth Management in the States.* Cambridge, Mass.: Lincoln Institute for Land Policy.

Duerksen, Christopher. 1983. *Environmental Regulation of Industrial Siting: How to Make It Work Better.* Washington, D.C.: Conservation Foundation.

Farr, James A., and O. Greg Brock. 2006. Florida's landmark programs for conservation and recreation land acquisition. http://www.dep.state.fl.us/lands/info/Florida%20Land%20Acquisition.doc (accessed August 7, 2008).

Gale, Dennis E. 1992. Eight state-sponsored growth management programs: A comparative analysis. *Journal of the American Planning Association* 58(4): 425–39.

Gammage, Grady. 1999. *Phoenix in Perspective.* Phoenix: Arizona State University, Herberger Center for Design.

Goetz, Stephan J. 2007. The economic case for state land use decision-making. *Journal of Regional Analysis and Policy* 37(1): 20–24.

Gray, Regina C. 2007. Ten years of smart growth: A nod to policies past and a prospective glimpse into the future. *Cityscape* 9(1): 109–30.

Hall, Bob, and Mary Lee Kerr. 1991. *1991–1992 Green Index.* Washington, D.C.: Island Press.

Higgins, Harrison, and Neil Paradise. 2007. Paying for the "priceless": Florida forever, managing growth, and public land acquisition. In *Growth Management in Florida: Planning for Paradise*, ed. T. Chapin, C. Connerly, and H. Higgins, 241–60. London: Ashgate Press.

Houstoun, Lawrence O., Jr., Paul R. Levy, Steve Gibson, and Howard Kozloff. 2003. *Business Improvement Districts*. Second Edition. Washington, D.C.: Urban Land Institute.

Jacobs, Harvey M. 2003. The politics of property rights at the national level: Signals and trends. *Journal of the American Planning Association* 69(2): 181–89.

———. 2005. Claiming the site: Evolving social-legal conceptions of ownership and property. In *Site Matters*, ed. C. Burns and A. Kahn, 19–37. New York: Routledge.

Lang, Robert E. 2007. Accidental cities. *Planning* (July): 42–47.

Lang, Robert E., and Jennifer B. LeFurgy. 2007. *Boomburbs: The Rise of America's Accidental Cities*. Washington, D.C.: Brookings Institution Press.

Lang, Robert E., and Arthur C. Nelson. 2007. America 2040: The rise of the megapolitans. *Planning* (January): 4–9.

Lang, Robert E., and Thomas Sanchez. 2007. Suburban blues: The democratic sweep to the metropolitan edge. Election Brief, Metropolitan Institute at Virginia Tech, Alexandria, Va.

Mason, Robert J. 2007. *Re-Placing Regulation: The Quieter Revolution in Land-Use Planning*. Lanham, Md.: Rowman & Littlefield.

Meck, Stuart, ed. 2002. *Growing Smart Legislative Guidebook: Model Statutes for Planning and the Management of Change*. Chicago: APA Planners Press.

Meyer, Stephen M. 1995. The economic impact of environmental regulation. *Journal of Environmental Law and Practice* 3(2): 4–15.

Nelson, Arthur C. 2000. Smart growth or business as usual? Which is better at improving quality of life and central city vitality? In *Making Regions Work for Everyone*, ed. Susan M. Wachter, R. Leo Penne, and Arthur C. Nelson, 82–105. Washington, D.C.: Office of Policy Development and Research, U.S. Department of Housing and Urban Development.

———. 2006. Planning in a new era. *Journal of the American Planning Association* 72(4): 393–407.

Nelson, Arthur C., and James B. Duncan with Clancy Mullen and Kirk Bishop. 1995. *Growth Management Principles and Practices*. Chicago: American Planning Association.